ENGLISH

KnowHow

Student Book Opener

Therese Naber · Angela Blackwell

with Michelle Johnstone

OXFORD
UNIVERSITY PRESS

Contents

Contents

Listening / Speaking	Reading / Writing	KnowHow
➤ **Listening:** Description of a neighborhood ➤ **Speaking:** Designing an ideal neighborhood	➤ **Reading:** • *Postcard* • *New Urbanism* ➤ **Writing:** An advertising brochure	➤ Listening tips
➤ **Speaking:** What can athletes do? ➤ **Listening:** A game show	➤ **Reading:** • *Instructor Profile* • *Amazing Athletes* ➤ **Writing:** Describing abilities	➤ Pronunciation of *can* and *can't*
➤ **Speaking:** • What are people doing? • Describing pictures ➤ **Listening:** Who can talk on the phone?	➤ **Reading:** *Home Phones* ➤ **Reading and Writing:** *The Message* – A TV script	➤ Spelling *-ing* forms
➤ **Listening:** • Weather in January • Song – "Blue Skies" ➤ **Speaking:** How do your clothes and activities change by season?	➤ **Reading:** *Traveling to Mars?* ➤ **Writing:** Life and seasons	➤ Sentence stress
➤ **Listening:** Computer Dos and Don'ts ➤ **Speaking:** Giving advice	➤ **Reading:** *Computers: How much is too much?* ➤ **Reading and Writing:** *Ask Jenna*—an advice column	➤ Organizing vocabulary
➤ **Listening:** Who did the letters belong to? ➤ **Speaking:** Where did you find the bottle?	➤ **Reading:** *A Message in a Bottle* ➤ **Writing:** A letter	➤ Pronunciation of *-ed* endings
➤ **Listening:** Justine Kerfoot's life story ➤ **Speaking:** Important dates and events in your life	➤ **Reading:** *A True Pioneer* ➤ **Writing:** A famous person	➤ Reading tips
➤ **Speaking:** Describing festivals in your country ➤ **Listening:** • Birthday presents • Song – "Celebration"	➤ **Reading:** • *Voices in the street* • *Festivals Around the World* ➤ **Writing:** Describing a festival	➤ Pronunciation of ordinal numbers

1 A world of words

✔ Introductions; names; nationalities
✔ Subject pronouns; the verb *be*

1 ▷ English Around You

a Do you recognize any English words in these pictures? Make a list.

b Make a list of other words you know in English. Then compare lists with a partner.

c Make a list of English words you see outside class. Bring your list to class and compare.

2 Language in Action: Introductions

a **AUDIO** Listen. Write the number of the correct conversation under each picture.

A ___   B ___   C ___

1 A: Hi, I'm Dave. What's your name?
  B: Hi, I'm Laura.

2 A: Hello, my name's Dana Webb. This is John Asakura.
  B: Nice to meet you. I'm Felipe Mendoza.
  C: Nice to meet you.

3 A: Hi, my name is Carla. I'm your tour guide.

b **AUDIO** Listen again. Cover the conversations above. Which conversations use the expressions below?

	1	2	3
Hi	✓		✓
Hello		✓	
Nice to meet you.			
My name's…			
I'm…			
This is…			
What's your name?			

c **AUDIO** Listen again. Practice the conversations. Use your own names.

d Introduce yourself to other students.

Example *Hi, I'm Luis. What's your name?*

3 ▶ In Conversation

AUDIO Who is from Canada? Who is from the United States? Listen. Then read.

Rita: Hi, my name's Rita.
Kelly: Hi, I'm Kelly. And this is Eric.
Eric: Hi! Where are you from, Rita?
Rita: I'm from Montreal, Canada.
Eric: Oh, you're Canadian. We're from the United States.
Rita: Yes, I know.
Eric: Oh, is it obvious?
Rita: Well…
Kelly: Oh, the name tags!

4 ▶ Vocabulary: Countries and nationalities

a **AUDIO** Listen and practice saying the words.

Country	Nationality	Country	Nationality
Brazil	Brazilian	Germany	German
Canada	Canadian	Mexico	Mexican
Colombia	Colombian	the United States	American
Norway	Norwegian	Korea	Korean
Italy	Italian	Kenya	Kenyan
China	Chinese	the United Kingdom	British
Japan	Japanese	Ireland	Irish
Lebanon	Lebanese	Spain	Spanish

b Work with a partner. Practice. **A**, say the name of a country. **B**, say the nationality of that country.

Example   **A:** *Mexico*
          B: *Mexican*

> ▼ **Help Desk**
>
> *Where are you from?*
> *I'm **from Canada**.*
> Or
> *I'm **Canadian**.*

5 ▶ *KnowHow*: Word stress

AUDIO Listen again. Mark the stress on the nationality words.

Example   *Brazílian*

Canadian   Chinese   German   British
Colombian   Japanese   Mexican   Irish
Norwegian   Lebanese   American   Spanish
Italian   Korean
                        Kenyan

6 ▶ Focus on Grammar

a Look at the chart. Fill in the blanks under the pictures with *You* or *We*.

Subject pronouns and *be* (affirmative)		
Singular	**Plural**	
I **am**	We **are**	
You **are**	You **are**	Canadian.
He **is** Canadian.	They **are**	
She **is**		
It **is**		

3

_____ are Canadian.

1

You are Canadian.

2

_____ are from the United States.

b Fill in the blanks with *am*, *is*, or *are*.

1 Eric is from the United States. He ____*is*____ American.
2 Carla is a tour guide. She _____ Brazilian.
3 We _____ tour guides.
4 My name is Eduardo. I _____ from Mexico.
5 It _____ a Japanese camera.
6 Mee Hye and Jung are from Korea. They _____ Korean.

▼ **Help Desk**

To form most plurals add **-s**.

one tour guide

*two or more tour guide**s***

c [AUDIO] Complete the chart. Then listen and practice the contractions.

Contractions with *be*								
I am	=	I'm	he is	=	he's	we are	=	we're
you are	=	_____	she is	=	_____	you are	=	you're
			it is	=	_____	they are	=	_____
Note:	Eric is	=	Eric's					

d Fill in the blanks. Use contractions.

1 Hi, I ___*'m*___ Felipe. What's your name?
2 It _____ a guitar.
3 Carla _____ a tour guide.
4 She _____ from Brazil.
5 They _____ tourists from the United States.

7 ▶ Speaking

a Choose the name of a famous person. Use that name and introduce "yourself" to other students.

Example A: *Hi, I'm….*
B: *Hi,…. I'm…. I'm from….*
Where are you from?
A: *I'm from….*

b Work with a partner. Try to remember names and places from 7a. Talk about the other students. Use *He's / She's / They're…*

8 ▶ Writing

a Complete the conversations with the expressions below.

| Hello. My name's Greg Soto. | Nice to meet you, Lisa. I'm Dan. |
| Anna. | Hi, Paul. I'm Louise. |

1 Hi, I'm Paul.
Hi, Paul. I'm Louise.

2 This is Lisa Cooper.
_____

3 What's your name?
_____

4 Hello. My name's Isabel Silva.
_____

b Write a conversation for picture A.

A: _____
_____

B: _____
_____

A: _____
_____

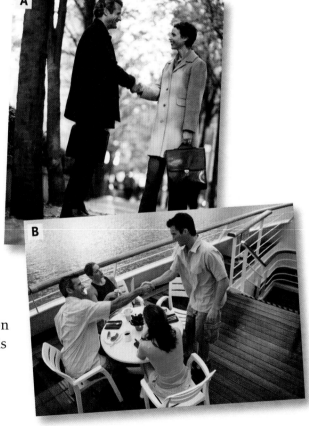

A

B

9 ▶ Listening

a AUDIO Listen. What are the names of the men in picture B?

Michael   Conor   Sarah   Chloe

b AUDIO Listen again. Which name is common in many different countries? Which name is common in Ireland?

10 ▶ Reading

a Read the article below about names in different countries.
Then answer the questions.

What is a common…
1 German name for a boy?
2 Japanese name for a girl?
3 Irish name for a girl?
4 Canadian name for a boy?

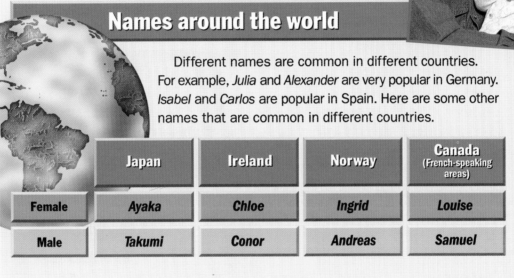

Names around the world

Different names are common in different countries.
For example, *Julia* and *Alexander* are very popular in Germany.
Isabel and *Carlos* are popular in Spain. Here are some other
names that are common in different countries.

	Japan	Ireland	Norway	Canada (French-speaking areas)
Female	*Ayaka*	*Chloe*	*Ingrid*	*Louise*
Male	*Takumi*	*Conor*	*Andreas*	*Samuel*

b Look at the article again. Which names do you like?

11 ▶ Speaking

a Write six common names in your country (three for a woman, three for a man).

Your country		
Female	Female	Female
Male	Male	Male

b Work as a group and compare answers. Which names are the most common?

2 Centered on language

✔ Personal information; spelling; classroom language
✔ Wh- questions; the verb be: Negative

1 ▶ Vocabulary: The alphabet and numbers 1–20

a AUDIO Look at the letters on the telephone keypad. Listen and practice saying the alphabet.

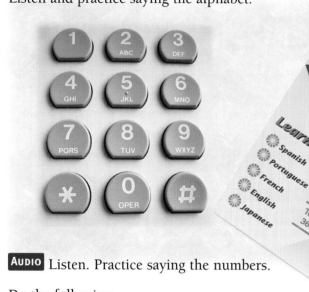

1	one	11	eleven
2	two	12	twelve
3	three	13	thirteen
4	four	14	fourteen
5	five	15	fifteen
6	six	16	sixteen
7	seven	17	seventeen
8	eight	18	eighteen
9	nine	19	nineteen
10	ten	20	twenty

b AUDIO Listen. Practice saying the numbers.

c Do the following:

1 Spell the name of the language center.
2 Say the phone number of the language center.
3 Spell your name.
4 Say your phone number.

2 ▶ In Conversation

AUDIO What language does Abby want to study? Listen. Then read.

Staff: Good morning. Uptown Language Center.
Abby: Hello. I'd like to register for a beginning Japanese class.
Staff: OK. What's your name?
Abby: Abby…Abby Klein.
Staff: How do you spell "Klein"?
Abby: K-L-E-I-N.
Staff: And what's your telephone number, please?
Abby: It's 463-8045. And my e-mail address is Abigail@net.khw.
Staff: OK. And your street address?
Abby: It's 17 Davis Avenue, apartment 12-D.
Staff: OK, that's everything.
Abby: Thank you. Goodbye.
Staff: Goodbye.

▼ **Help Desk**

Saying e-mail addresses:
@ = *at*   . = *dot*

7

3 ▶ Vocabulary: Personal information

a Match 1–5 to an item from a–e.

1	a last name	*1c*	a	Abigail@net.khw
2	a street address	—	b	intermediate
3	an e-mail address	—	c	Klein
4	a telephone number	—	d	463-8045
5	a class level	—	e	17 Davis Avenue

b Circle the correct answer in parentheses. Then fill in the blanks 1–4 with *a* or *an*.

Use *an* before a (consonant / vowel sound).

1 _____ apartment
2 _____ name
3 _____ language class
4 _____ address

4 ▶ Focus on Grammar

a Look at the chart. Which question is the same in the singular and plural?

Wh- questions (information questions) with be	
Singular	*Plural*
What **is** your name?	What **are** your names?
Where **are** you from?	Where **are** you from?
Where **is** Abby from?	Where **are** Abby and Brad from?
Where **is** the beginning Spanish class?	Where **are** the Spanish classes?

Note: Contractions
What is → What's   Where is → Where's
What are / Where are → no contraction

b Write questions.

1 What / your name   *What is your name?* _____
2 What / your address   _____
3 Where / the teacher from _____
4 Where / the language classes _____
5 Where / the English class _____
6 What / your phone number _____
7 What / your e-mail address _____
8 Where / you from   _____

8

5 ▶ Language in Action: Asking for clarification

a **AUDIO** Listen and practice.

> A: What's your last name?
> B: Klein.
> A: How do you spell "Klein"?
> B: K-L-E-I-N.
> A: Can you repeat that, please?
> B: Yes, it's K-L-E-I-N.

> • How do you spell…?
> • Can you repeat that?

b Work with a partner. Practice the conversation with your own names.

c Find three words from Unit 1. Ask your partner *How do you spell…?*

> Example   A: *How do you spell "Japanese"?*
>   B: *J-A-P-A-N-E-S-E.*

6 ▶ Listening

AUDIO Listen and complete the form.

Register Here
For
Spanish Classes

A **Registration form: Uptown Language Center**

Name: Brad ¹ _____

Address: ² _____   Monroe Street _____

            Apartment ³ _____

Telephone: ⁴ _____

E-mail: ⁵ _____ @net.khw _____

Language: English French Japanese Portuguese Spanish

Level: Beginning   Intermediate   Advanced

7 ▶ Writing and Speaking

a Work with a partner. Ask your partner questions from 4b on page 8. Complete form B. Then change roles.

b Look at your partner's form. Is the information about you correct?

B **Registration form: Uptown Language Center**

Name: _____

Address: _____

            _____

Telephone: _____

E-mail: _____

Language: English French Japanese Portuguese Spanish

Level: Beginning   Intermediate   Advanced

In Conversation

AUDIO Is Brad in the correct class? Listen. Then read.

Brad: Excuse me.
Teacher: Yes?
Brad: What class is this? Is it beginning Spanish?
Teacher: No, this isn't beginning Spanish. This is advanced Spanish.
Brad: Oh, good!
Teacher: Good?
Brad: Yes, I'm glad this isn't my class. I don't understand anything!

9 Focus on Grammar

a Look at the chart. Find two examples of the negative in the conversation above.

The verb *be*: Negative (full forms and contractions)		
I **am not**	I**'m not**	
You **are not**	You **aren't** (You**'re not**)	
He / She / It **is not**	He / She / It **isn't** (He / She / It**'s not**)	in my class.
We **are not**	We **aren't** (We**'re not**)	
You **are not**	They **aren't** (They**'re not**)	

b **AUDIO** Fill in the blanks with negative contractions. Listen and check.

1 Class 1 _isn't_ in Room 7.

2 You _____ in Room 3.

3 Stephen and Sophie _____ English teachers.

4 I _____ in the Advanced English Class.

c Write pairs of sentences. What <u>isn't</u> correct on Class List A?

Example
1) *Class 1 isn't Advanced English. It's Intermediate English.*
2) *It isn't in room 9. It's in room 11.*

CLASS LIST A

Class 1
¹Advanced English
²Room 9
³Teacher: Daniel

Class 2
Advanced Japanese
⁴Room 14
⁵Teacher: Lisa

Class 3
⁶Intermediate French
Room 3
⁷Teachers: Caroline and Thierry

FINAL CLASS LIST

Class 1
Intermediate English
Room 11
Teacher: Linda

Class 2
Advanced Japanese
Room 7
Teacher: Mari

Class 3
Beginning French
Room 3
Teachers:
Stephen and Sophie

10 ▶ Speaking

Work with a partner. A, write three or four sentences about yourself. Make one sentence <u>false</u>. B, find the false sentence and correct it.

Example   A: *My phone number is 682-1045.*
                B: *Your phone number isn't 682-1045.*
                    It's 682-1099.

11 ▶ *KnowHow*: Classroom language

a **AUDIO** Listen. Number the instructions in the order you hear them.

Open your books. ___

Close your books. ___

Work with a partner. ___

Listen to the conversation. ___

Read the directions. ___

Say *student*. _1_

Write *student* in your notebook. ___

b Work with a partner. Look at Units 1 and 2. Add three more instructions to the list.

1   *Make a list.* _____
2   _____
3   _____
4   _____

12 ▶ Reading and Speaking

a Read the article and the graph. What are the two most important uses for English in the graph?

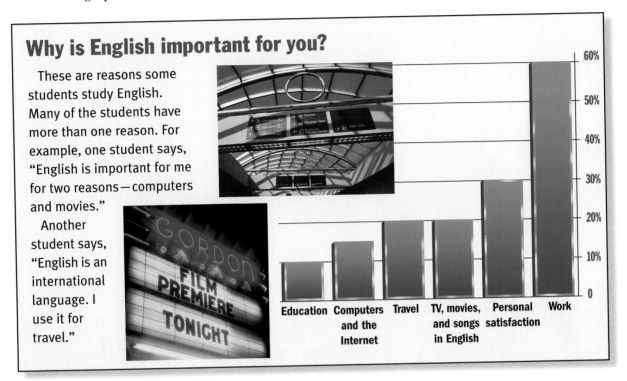

Why is English important for you?

These are reasons some students study English. Many of the students have more than one reason. For example, one student says, "English is important for me for two reasons—computers and movies."

Another student says, "English is an international language. I use it for travel."

b Ask three students *Why is English important for you?* Fill in the blanks (1–3) with their names. Then check (✓) their answers.

Names	1 _____	2 _____	3 _____
1 Work			
2 Personal satisfaction			
3 TV / movies / songs			
4 Travel			
5 Computers / Internet			
6 Education			

c Calculate the totals for the class. Make a graph like the one in 12a with the totals.

Class Total	
1 Work	
2 Personal satisfaction	
3 TV / movies / songs	
4 Travel	
5 Computers / Internet	
6 Education	

3 Take note!

✔ Signs and messages; time; numbers; polite expressions
✔ Imperatives; possessive forms

1 Reading

a Read the messages and signs (1–5). Then match them with the correct pictures (A–E).

Please Close the Door

Come to a Party!

message
Call Ann.
Her number is
389-6521

MEMO
To: All managers
Re: Sales meeting

Meeting at 3 p.m.
Please, don't be
late!

1 ___   2 ___   3 ___   4 ___   5 ___

b AUDIO Listen. Write the number of the items you hear. — — —

2 Speaking

a How do you communicate? Put the media in order (1–4) for each situation.
(1 = most often, 4 = least often)

	by telephone	by e-mail	by handwritten messages	face-to-face
with family				
with friends				
at work				

b Compare your answers with other students. Are your answers similar or different?

3 ▶ Vocabulary: Action verbs

a Write pairs of verbs.

sit   walk   open   read   come   write   stand   go   close   run

1   _sit_   _stand_   4   _____   _____
2   _____   _____   5   _____   _____
3   _____   _____

b Compare your answers with other students.

4 ▶ Focus on Grammar

a Look at the chart. Then find three more imperatives in section 1.

Imperatives	
Affirmative	*Negative*
Walk.	**Don't** walk.
Call Ann.	**Don't** call Ann.

b Write the signs below the correct pictures.

Please don't sit on the grass

Do not open this window

Go slow

WALK. DON'T RUN

PRIVATE Do not enter

Don't park here

Please be quiet

Put books here

1   _Please don't sit on the grass_   5   _____
2   _____   6   _____
3   _____   7   _____
4   _____   8   _____

5 Vocabulary: Numbers 20–100 and time

a AUDIO Try to complete the chart. Listen and check your answers.

Numbers 20-100

twenty	20	--	25	thirty	30	eighty	80
twenty-one	21	twenty-six	26	forty	40	ninety	90
--	22	--	27	fifty	50	one hundred	100
twenty-three	23	twenty-eight	28	sixty	60		
twenty-four	24	--	29	seventy	70		

b AUDIO Listen. Practice saying the times.

1

It's eleven o'clock.

3

It's a quarter to one.
It's twelve forty-five.

5

It's two thirty.

2

It's twenty-five after nine.
It's nine twenty-five.

4

It's five to seven.
It's six fifty-five.

6

It's a quarter after ten.
It's ten fifteen.

c What time…

1 is your class?
2 is your favorite television show?
3 is it now?

6 KnowHow: Pronunciation of numbers

a AUDIO Listen. Which number do you hear?

1	14	40	4	13	30
2	19	90	5	15	50
3	16	60	6	18	80

b Work with a partner. **A**, say one number from each pair of numbers in 6a. **B**, write the number. Check your answers. Then change roles.

> ▼ **Help Desk**
>
> *noon* = 12 o'clock (day)
> *midnight* = 12 o'clock (night)
> *a.m.* = from midnight until noon
> *p.m.* = from noon until midnight

Language in Action: Polite expressions

a **AUDIO** What do you think the man on the left is asking about? Listen and check your answer.

b **AUDIO** Complete the conversation with expressions from the box below. Then listen again and check.

Person 1: ¹*Excuse me.* _____

What time is it, ²_____?

Person 2: ³_____. I don't know.

Person 3: It's 5 o'clock.

Person 1: ⁴_____.

Person 3: ⁵_____.

c Practice the conversation. Use these times.

1 6:00   2 3:20   3 4:45   4 (the time now)

POLITE EXPRESSIONS

- I'm sorry.
- Please
- You're welcome.
- Excuse me.
- Thank you

Listening

a **AUDIO** Look at the agenda. Listen. Practice saying the days of the week.

AGENDA

Sunday _____

_____

Monday _____

_____

Tuesday _____

_____

Wednesday _____

_____

Thursday _____

_____

Friday *Tennis at 4*

_____

Saturday _____

_____

☎ **MESSAGES**

Matt,

1. Alex called. Tennis on a) *Friday* at b) *4* o'clock.

2. Vanessa called. Dinner is at The Grand Café at c) ___ o'clock tonight.

3. Dr. Landau on d) _____ at e) ___ o'clock

4. It isn't The Grand Café, it's The Modern Café. Call Jack for the address. His number is f) _____.

b **AUDIO** Listen to Matt's messages. Check the items you hear.

1 tennis ___   4 dinner ___
2 football ___   5 doctor ___
3 lunch ___

c **AUDIO** Listen again. Complete the messages in 8a for Matt.

d What is the problem with Matt's schedule?

▼ **Help Desk**

Use *on* with days of the week and *at* with times.

*The meeting is **on** Tuesday **at** 10:00 a.m.*

16

9 ▸ Focus on Grammar

a Look at the messages. Then complete the chart.

Possessive adjectives and possessive 's

Possessive adjectives		Possessive 's
I	*my*	Jack**'s** number is 248-9053.
you	*your*	Vanessa**'s** address is 23 Ellis Street.
he	_____	Dan and Ling**'s** address is 72 Grant Avenue.
she	_____	
we	*our*	
they		

b **AUDIO** Listen and practice the pronunciation of the possessive 's.

Jack's   Vanessa's   Liz's   Mitch's

What's…phone number?

c Fill in the blanks.

1   ___*My*___ name's Karen. I live in Los Angeles.
2   _____ name's Matthew, but everyone calls him "Matt."
3   We live in an apartment. _____ address is
    93 Elm Street.
4   What's _____ name?
    —I think it's Diana, but I'm not sure.
5   Is _____ phone number 379-1872?
    —Yes, that's my number.

d Look at the pictures. Match the people and their addresses.
Then make sentences.

Nicholas

Roger and Simone

Melanie

simro@us.khw   12 Hill Street, Apt. 2   nick@123.khw   60 Wood Road, Apt. 33
                      mel.p@pal.khw   82 Maple Avenue

Example   *Melanie's address is 60 Wood Road, Apt. 33.*
          Her e-mail address is…

Handwritten notes:

Call Vanessa.
Her number is
379-1872.

Call Dan and Ling.
Their number is
504-9306.

Jack's address is
68 Prince Avenue.

His e-mail address
is Jack68@net.khw

10 ▶ Writing: E-mail messages

a Read the e-mail messages. Number them in the correct order.

From: Vanessa@pdq.khw
To: matthew@net.khw
Subject: Re: Dinner

Hi Matt,
I'm sorry. It isn't The Grand Café.
It's The Modern Café. Thursday at 7.
Don't be late. OK?
Vanessa ☐

From: matthew@net.khw
To: Vanessa@pdq.khw
Subject: Re: Dinner

Hi Vanessa,
OK. The Modern Café at 7 o'clock.
I'm never late!
Matt ☐

From: Vanessa@pdq.khw
To: matthew@net.khw
Subject: Dinner

Hi Matt,
Meet me at The Grand Café for dinner
on Thursday at 7 o'clock. OK? The
address is 50 Summit Street.
Vanessa ☐1☐

From: matthew@net.khw
To: Vanessa@pdq.khw
Subject: Re: Dinner

Hi Vanessa,
Great! Thank you. See you at The
Grand Café on Thursday at 7 o'clock.
Matt ☐

---

b Work in pairs. Write an e-mail to your partner. Use the information on the calendar (or your own ideas).

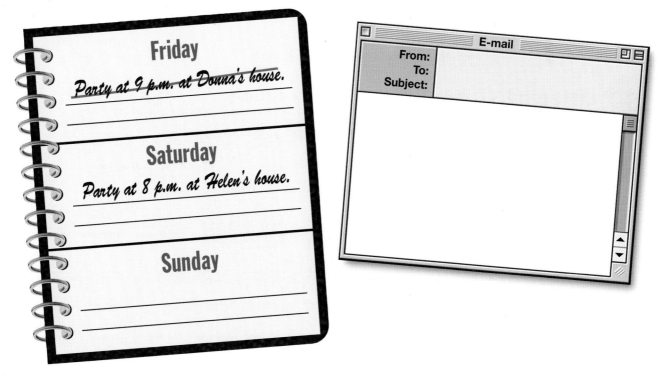

Friday
Party at 9 p.m. at Donna's house.

Saturday
Party at 8 p.m. at Helen's house.

Sunday

| E-mail |
| From: |
| To: |
| Subject: |

c Exchange messages. Answer your partner's e-mail.

4 Familiar things

✔ Everyday objects; jobs
✔ *This* / *these*; plural nouns; *yes* / *no* questions with *be*

1 ▸ Vocabulary: Jobs and objects

a **AUDIO** Look at the pictures. Listen and practice saying the words.

businessperson

police officer

waiter

teacher

construction worker

doctor and nurse

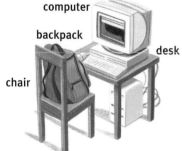
computer
backpack
desk
chair

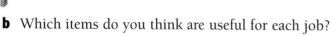
notebook
pen
pencil

address book

mug

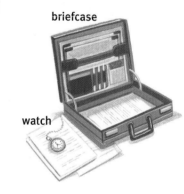
briefcase
watch

b Which items do you think are useful for each job?

2 ▸ Listening

a **AUDIO** Listen. Number the people in the order you hear them.

Teacher ___   Construction worker ___   Doctor ___

b **AUDIO** Listen again. Which items are useful or not useful for each person?

	desk/chair	pen/pencil	notebook	address book	computer	mug	briefcase	watch	backpack
Teacher									
Doctor									
Construction worker									

c Which items in section 1 are useful for you...

1 at work?   2 at home?

19

3 ▶ Focus on Grammar

a   Look at the chart and answer the questions.

   Is *this* singular or plural? And *these*?

This, These		**Plural nouns**
What's **this**?	What are **these**?	book + **s** = books
		class + **es** = classes
It's a book.	**They**'re books.	watch + **es** = watches
It's an address book.	**They**'re address books.	**Note:** For words that end in **s** or a similar sound,
It's a watch.	**They**'re watches.	such as *ch, sh, ss*, add *–es* to form the plural.

b   **AUDIO** Fill in the blanks. Then listen and practice.

1   What *'s this*_____?
    *It's a*_____ desk.

2   What _____?
    _____ English book.

3   What _____?
    _____ notebooks.

4   What _____?
    _____ computer.

5   What _____?
    _____ briefcases.

6   What _____?
    _____ coffee mugs.

4 ▶ *KnowHow* : Remembering vocabulary

a   Do you remember the names of these objects? It's easy to forget new vocabulary.
   4b is a memory game to help you.

b   Work with a partner. Look at the vocabulary on page 19 for thirty seconds. Then close
   your books and try to write as many words as you can.

20

5 Language in Action: Useful questions

a AUDIO Work with a partner. Listen and practice the conversations.

1 A: What's this in English?
   B: It's an umbrella.
   A: How do you spell "umbrella"?
   B: U-M-B-R-E-L-L-A.

2 A: What are these in English?
   B: They're keys.
   A: How do you spell "keys"?
   B: K-E-Y-S.

b Work with a partner. **A**, ask questions about the things in the bag. **B**, answer the questions. Use questions from 5a.

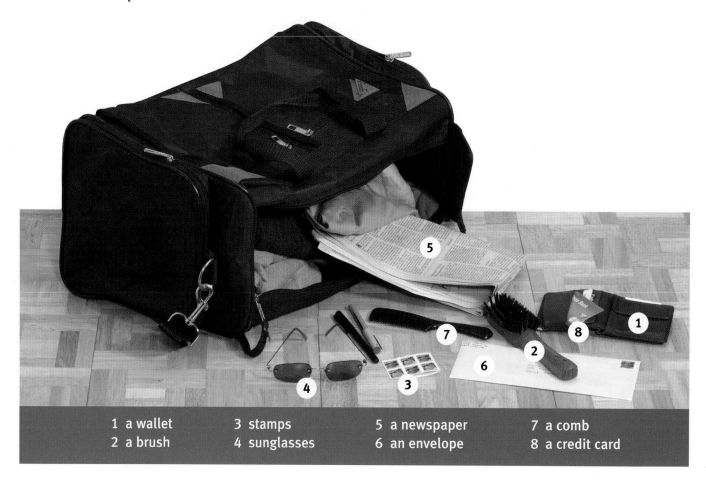

1 a wallet	3 stamps	5 a newspaper	7 a comb
2 a brush	4 sunglasses	6 an envelope	8 a credit card

6 ▶ In Conversation

AUDIO What are their jobs? Listen. Then read.

Man: Excuse me, is this your stethoscope?
Woman: Oh yes, it is. Thank you very much.
Man: You're welcome. Are you a doctor?
Woman: Yes, I am. Are you an artist?
Man: No, I'm a teacher. Why?
Woman: Because of the things in your bag.
Man: Oh. I'm on my way to my art class.

7 ▶ Focus on Grammar

a Look at the chart. Find an example of a *yes / no* question in the conversation above.

Yes / No questions with be

Questions	Answers	
Are you a teacher?	Yes, I **am**.	No, **I'm not**.
Is he / she a teacher?	Yes, he / she **is**.	No, he / she **isn't**.
Is it a computer?	Yes, it **is**.	No, it **isn't**.
Are they artists?	Yes, they **are**.	No, they **aren't**.

b Write questions using these words.

1 you / an artist   *Are you an artist?* _____
2 this / your pen   _____
3 Christopher / a doctor   _____
4 Lucy / a police officer   _____
5 Gwen and Maya / teachers   _____
6 these / your newspapers   _____

c Now, match these answers to the questions in 7b.

a Yes, he is.   3
b No, I'm not.   —
c No, they aren't. They're nurses.   —
d Yes, they are.   —
e Yes, she is.   —
f Yes, it is. Thanks.   —

d Work in groups. Put one or two objects (a pen, a notebook) in the middle of the table. Then choose an object and ask questions.

Example   **A:** *David, is this your notebook?*
                B: *No, it isn't.*
                A: *Angela, is this your notebook?*
                C: *Yes, it is.*

Vocabulary: Location

a Look at the examples of the prepositions.

in   on   under   next to

b Look at the picture. Complete the sentences.
  Use *in, on, under,* or *next to.*

1 The backpack is *on the table*_____.
2 The notebook is _____.
3 The pens are _____.
4 The chair is _____.
5 The cat is _____.

 Speaking

Work with a partner. Look at the pictures and
find six differences.

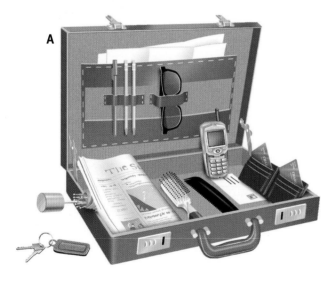

A

B

Example *The umbrella is under the
        newspaper in picture A. It's on
        the newspaper in picture B.*

10 ▶ Reading

a Read and match each description with a picture of a desk.

1

Patricia

My desk isn't really a desk. It's our family table. It isn't very neat. All kinds of things are on it—papers, newspapers, my briefcase, the telephone, and an umbrella. Oh, and it's also our cat's favorite place. A lot of things are on the desk, but it isn't easy to find them!

A ___

2

Edwin

My desk is very neat. My favorite pen and notebook are always on the desk. The telephone is right next to the computer. The telephone and the computer are very important for my work. As you can see, a picture of my family is on the desk, too. Everything is in perfect order.

B ___

3

Nate

My desk is messy. I'm not very organized. My books and papers are all over my desk. My coffee mug is on the papers. I drink a lot of coffee when I study.

C ___

b Read again. Which person mentions each thing?

favorite pen　family table　coffee　family picture　books　briefcase

Example　*favorite pen—Edwin*

11 ▶ Writing

a What is your desk at home or work like? Is it messy or neat? Write a description of your desk.

b Compare your description with your classmates' descriptions. How many are messy? Neat?

Grammar

Tour Schedule

LOS ANGELES

Sunday:	2:30 p.m.	Orientation meeting
Monday:	9:15 a.m.	Tour: Los Angeles
	1:45 p.m.	Tour: Hollywood
	7:30 p.m.	Dinner
Tuesday:	8:00 a.m.	Tour: Film studios
	12:00 p.m.	Lunch
	2:15 p.m.	Shopping trip
	6:15 p.m.	Goodbye party

1 Write T (true) or F (false). Correct the false statements.

1 The orientation meeting is on Monday.
   _F_   _The meeting is on Sunday._

2 On Monday, the tour of Los Angeles is at nine forty-five.
   __   _____

3 The tour of Hollywood is at a quarter after two.
   __   _____

4 On Tuesday, lunch is at noon.
   __   _____

5 The goodbye party is on Thursday at a quarter to six.
   __   _____

2 Put the words in the correct order. Write imperative statements.

1 do / the windows / open / not
   Do not open the windows.

2 don't / after 11 p.m. / call
   _____

3 please / bags / your / here / put
   _____

3 Complete the conversation with *am / 'm, is / 's,* or *are / 're.*

> Good morning. My name is Scott and I am your tour guide. Please say hello to the people next to you.

Clara: Hello, I'm Clara Andersen. And this ___*is*___ ¹ Gilbert Sanders.

Hans: My name _____ ² Hans Gertz. I'm from Germany. Where _____ ³ you from, Clara?

Clara: I _____ ⁴ from Norway. Gilbert _____ ⁵ from Canada. We _____ ⁶ teachers.

4 Complete the conversation with *I, you, he, we,* or *they.*

Wendy: Hi, I'm Wendy. ¹ ___*I*___ 'm from Ireland. Oh, and meet Amanda and Alessandro Oliveira. ² _____ 're from Brazil.

Ingrid: Nice to meet you, Amanda and Alessandro. Are ³ _____ from Rio?

Amanda: No, ⁴ _____ 're from São Paulo.

Wendy: And that's Fred Hanks.

Amanda: ⁵ _____ 's from the United Kingdom. He's a police officer.

5 Write true sentences about the tourists.

Example   Hans is Mexican.
          Hans isn't Mexican. He's German.

1 Amanda and Alessandro are German.
   _____

2 Wendy is Japanese.
   _____

3 Fred is Canadian.
   _____

6 Write *yes / no* questions and answers with *be*. Look at exercises 3 and 4 for the information.

1 Fred / businessman
   Is Fred a businessman?
   No, he isn't. He's a police officer.

2 Amanda / from Rio
   _____
   _____

3 Clara and Gilbert / business people
   _____
   _____

7 Fill in the blanks with the possessive forms *my, your, his, her, our,* or *their.*

1 Celia, ¹ *your* credit cards are on the table.
   —Oh! ² _____ credit cards! Thank you.

2 Celia is an artist. ³ _____ pictures are great!

3 Amanda and Alessandro, is this a photo of ⁴ _____ family?
   —Yes, it is. These are ⁵ _____ four children.

4 Look, a photo of Amanda, Alessandro, and ⁶ _____ children. It's a nice photo.

5 Tell Fred that ⁷ _____ computer is under the table.

8 Write the questions.

1 *What's your last name?*
   My last name is Gertz.

2 _____
   G - E - R - T - Z.

3 _____
   It's herrhans@euronet.khw.

4 _____
   My phone number is 862-0539.

Vocabulary

9 Look at the objects below. Make two lists. Use *a* or *an* with the singular words.

Singular	Plural
a mug	sunglasses
an address book	

10 Complete the letter sets (1–5) with the letters below. Hint: Which letters have similar sounds?

   b u j x y f v m p

   1 a k __   4 c e t __ __ __
   2 i __   5 l n s __ __ __
   3 q w __

Six letters are missing. What are they?

Fun Spot

Days of the week

Write the names of days that have…

1 two Es (1): *Wednesday*
2 an S (5): _____
3 a T (3): _____
4 a U (4): _____
5 an R (3): _____

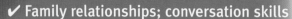

✔ Family relationships; conversation skills
✔ Simple present: Statements and *yes* / *no* questions

1 Vocabulary: Family relationships

a Look at the picture and read the family description.

b Try to fill in the blanks with the correct words. Which person is describing the picture?

brother   sister   mother   husband   parents

This is a picture from a party for my
¹ *parents*_____. They are in the center.
Mary is my ² _____ and Lawrence is
my father. This is my sister. Her name is Patti.
And this is my ³ _____ Calvin. This
is Roger. He's my husband. We have two children.
Kyra is our daughter and Danny is our son. Then,
there's Aunt Loretta. She's my father's
⁴ _____. Her ⁵ _____,
Uncle Kevin, isn't in the picture. And, finally, this
is my sister-in-law Miranda in the corner. She's
Calvin's wife.

c **AUDIO** Listen and check your answers. Then, practice saying the family words.

d Work with a partner. **A**, say the name of someone in Elaine's family.
B, describe that person. Use family words.

Example   A: *Kyra*
          B: *She's Roger and Elaine's daughter. She's Danny's sister.*

e Work with a partner. Write the names of three people in your family. Your partner asks
about the family relationship.

Example   A: *Sandra   Michael   Louis*
          B: *Is Sandra your wife?*
          A: *No, she isn't.*
          B: *Is she your sister?*
          A: *Yes, she is.*
          B: *Is Michael your brother?*

▼ **Help Desk**

Add *-in-law* for relationships
by marriage.

The sister of your husband or wife
= *sister-in-law*

The brother of your husband or wife
= *brother-in-law*

2 Reading

a Look at the pictures of the family reunions. Why do you think people have family reunions?

b Read the magazine article. What do these people like about family reunions?

Family Reunions

Many people live far away from family these days. So, family reunions are popular. People invite family from all over the country, or even the world. Here are comments from some of *your* family reunions.

Joanna:

I love our family reunions. My husband and I don't have children, but I have six nieces and four nephews. It's nice to see the whole family. My husband likes the reunions too. He has a very small family. His family doesn't have reunions.

Brandon:

I live in Hawaii, and I don't see my family a lot. I have one sister, Michelle, but I don't have brothers. I'm not married either. It's fun to see my family, especially my aunts, uncles, and cousins, at the family reunion. I don't see them often. But, I'm glad we only have reunions once a year. I'm happy to get back to Hawaii.

Jeff:

I'm 78 years old. I have four children and ten grandchildren. I live in Miami, but my children and grandchildren all live in different places, from California, to France, to Jamaica! I don't see them often. It's wonderful to have a reunion.

c Match the family relationships (1–5) with the correct family words (a–e).

1	Your parents' parents	_1e_	a niece
2	Your children's children	___	b nephew
3	Your aunt's or uncle's children	___	c cousins
4	Your brother's or sister's daughter	___	d grandchildren (or grandson and granddaughter)
5	Your brother's or sister's son	___	e grandparents (or grandmother and grandfather)

d Read the article again. Write the name of the person who talks about each item.

1 a husband   *Joanna*
2 one sister   _____
3 Hawaii   _____
4 ten grandchildren   _____
5 six nieces   _____
6 Miami   _____

e When and where do you see people in your family? Do you have special "family reunions"?

3 ▶ Focus on Grammar

a Look at the chart. Answer the questions.

1 When do you add -s to the verb?
2 When do you use *doesn't*?

Simple present: Statements

Affirmative		*Negative*	
I **live**		I **don't live**	
You **live**		You **don't live**	
He / She **lives**	in Miami.	He / She **doesn't live**	in Miami.
We **live**		We **don't live**	
They **live**		They **don't live**	

Note: The spelling changes with *he / she / it* for some verbs.

have ---▸ **has**   He **has** a sister.
go ---▸ **goes**   She **goes** to work.

b Circle the correct form.

1 Molly (have / has) one brother.
2 Her brother (live / lives) in Canada.
3 Kate and Peter (have / has) two children.
4 Nick's wife (have / has) a lot of cousins.
5 Their children (live / lives) in a different city.
6 We (don't / doesn't) live in New York.
7 Timmy doesn't (have / has) a brother.

> ▼ **Help Desk**
>
> In the simple present, remember to add -s to verbs with *he / she / it* in affirmative statements.
>
> *He lives in Canada.*

c Complete the paragraph with the correct forms of *live* or *have*.

My name is Patrick. I ¹ <u>   live   </u> in Monterrey, in Mexico. My parents ² _____ in Monterrey, too. I'm not married. I ³ _____ one brother and one sister. They ⁴ _____ (not) in Monterrey. My brother's name is Arturo and he ⁵ _____ in Mexico City. He is married, but he ⁶ _____ (not) children. My sister's name is Victoria. She's married and she ⁷ _____ two daughters. She ⁸ _____ (not) a son. She and her family live in Dallas, Texas.

d Write sentences about your family. Try to use all the words below.

is / isn't   have / has   live / lives   don't / doesn't

Examples *I live in Osaka. I have one sister and two brothers. My sister's name is Makiko. She lives in Yokohama. She isn't married. She has…*

Read another student's sentences. Are all the verbs formed correctly?

4 ▶ In Conversation

AUDIO Does Anna have brothers or sisters? Listen. Then read.

Anna: Do you have family here in Los Angeles?
Trish: No, I don't. My family lives in Arizona. In Phoenix, actually. Do you have family in Los Angeles?
Anna: Yes, my parents live here.
Trish: Do you have brothers or sisters?
Anna: Yes, I do. I have one brother.
Trish: Does he live here?
Anna: Yes, he does. Hey, you should meet him. He's a nice guy.
Trish: I don't know.
Anna: Oh, come on. He's really nice.
Trish: Well, maybe.

5 ▶ Focus on Grammar

a Look at the chart. Complete the sentences.

1 Use *do* with *I*, _____, *we*, and *they*.
2 Use *does* with _____, *she*, and *it*.

Simple present: *Yes / No* questions		
Questions	**Answers**	
Do you **have** brothers or sisters? **Does** he **live** here?	Yes, I **do**. Yes, he **does**.	No, I **don't**. No, he **doesn't**.

b Circle the correct word. Then answer the questions.

1 (Do / Does) Anna's parents live in Los Angeles?
2 (Do / Does) Anna have a sister?
3 (Do / Does) Anna's brother live in Los Angeles?
4 (Do / Does) Trish's family live in Los Angeles?

> ▼ *Help Desk*
>
> Remember not to add an *-s* to the verb after *does*.
>
> *Does she live in Brazil?*

c Use the chart below. Make at least five questions. Then interview another student.

Example *Do you live in an apartment?*

Do Does	you your (parents / sister, etc.) he / she they	live have	in an apartment? in a house? in Paris? in Tokyo? children? brothers? sisters? a dog? a cat? a car? a bicycle?

KnowHow: Intonation in yes / no questions

a **AUDIO** Listen to these questions. Notice how the voice goes up at the end of *yes / no* questions.

    1 Do you live in Tokyo?

    2 Do you live in an apartment?

    3 Does your sister have children?

b Now practice the questions.

7 **Listening**

a **AUDIO** Listen to the conversation. Number the topics in the order you hear them.

grandparents	—
parents	*1*
brothers / sisters	—
holidays	—
China	—

b **AUDIO** Listen again. Write T (true) or F (false).

    1 Ted's parents are from China.   —

    2 His mother's parents live in San Francisco.   —

    3 His father's parents live in San Francisco, too.   —

    4 He has two sisters.   —

    5 His sisters live in San Diego.   —

    6 He sees his family on holidays.   —

8 ▶ Language in Action: Starting a conversation

a Match the questions (1–4) with the correct responses (a–d).

1 Are you from around here?   _1b_   a No, I know his girlfriend, Katie.
2 Do you have family here?   —   b No, I'm not. I'm from Chicago.
3 Are you a friend of Ted's?   —   c Yes, it is. What about you?
4 Is this your first time here?   —   d No, I don't. My family lives in Arizona.

b **AUDIO** Listen and check your answers. Then practice.

c Work with a partner. Imagine you're in a social situation (for example, a party). Start a conversation and ask questions to keep it going. Try to continue for at least one minute.

> **▼ Help Desk**
>
> If someone asks you a question in a social situation, try to say more than *Yes* or *No*. Give some additional information. Then you can say *What about you?*

9 ▶ Speaking

Work in groups and discuss the questions. Use the words on the list.

every day   once a week   every weekend   once a month

How often do you…
1 talk to family on the phone?   3 celebrate a family occasion?
2 have lunch or dinner with family?   4 visit family in another city?

10 ▶ Writing

a Read the paragraphs about Ted.

Ted lives in Seattle. His parents are from Guangdong Province in China. They live in San Francisco now. His father's parents and other relatives live in China.

He has two sisters. Their names are Rita and Karen. Rita lives in San Francisco and Karen lives in San Diego. Rita is married and has one daughter. Karen is not married.

Ted goes to San Francisco once a month. When he is there, he has lunch or dinner with his family every day. He always sees his family on holidays.

b Write a similar text about another student's family. Use the information from your discussion in section 9.

6 Buying power

✔ Clothing; shopping; requests with *can*
✔ Demonstratives; *How much...?* + prices

1 ▶ Speaking

a How often do you shop for these things? Put the things in order.
(1 = most often, 5 = least often)

a. clothes ___

b. books ___

c. food ___

d. CDs ___

e. computer / electrical items ___

b Discuss your answers with other students.

Example *For me, food is number 1...*

2 ▶ Vocabulary: Colors

a **AUDIO** Listen and practice saying the colors.

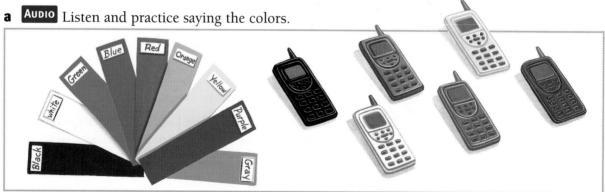

White Green Blue Red Orange Yellow Purple Black Gray

b Look at the pictures. Which cell phone colors are available? Which three colors are <u>not</u> available?

c Look at the pictures in 1a again. Find examples of as many colors as you can.

3 ▶ In Conversation

AUDIO What does the customer need? Listen. Then read.

1 **Customer:** Hello. Do you speak English?
　Clerk: Yes, I do. Can I help you?
Customer: Yes, please. I need a cable.
　Clerk: For your printer?
Customer: No, for my laptop computer.
　Clerk: Well, that's a printer cable, but this cable is for laptops.
Customer: OK, thank you.

2 **Customer:** Oh, I also need a camera.
　Clerk: What about one of those cameras over there? That small one is nice.
Customer: Hmmm…yes, it is. Can I see it, please?
　Clerk: Yes, sure. Oh, it needs batteries! Let's see. These are OK, I think…

4 ▶ Focus on Grammar

a Read the sentences in the chart. Find two examples of similar sentences in section 3.

▼ **Help Desk**

Use *over there* for something you can see, but not touch.

Demonstratives: *this, that, these, those*

	Singular	Plural	
	This cable is for a computer. **This** is a computer cable.	**These** cables are for computers. **These** are computer cables.	
	That cable is for a printer. **That** is a printer cable.	**Those** cables are for printers. **Those** are printer cables.	

---

b Look at the picture. Fill in the blanks with *this, that, these,* or *those.*

Excuse me, I need…
1 _*that*_ computer magazine.
2 _____ pen.
3 _____ newspapers.
4 _____ notebook.
5 _____ computer cables.

34

5 Vocabulary: Clothes

a **AUDIO** Listen. Look at the ad for CTS Stores. Number the clothes in the order you hear them.

CTS Stores

jacket $59.99 ___

sweater $29.99 ___

jeans $24.99 ___

MEN'S

shorts $21.99 ___

hat $14.99 ___

shirt $24.99 ___

boots $79.99 ___

tie $19.99 ___

suit $99.99 _1_

socks $7.50 ___

pants $39.99 ___

T-shirt $10.99 ___

skirt $34.99 ___

dress $49.99 ___

shoes $39.99 ___

WOMEN'S

b Now practice saying the words.

6 Speaking

Discuss these questions with other students.

1 What do you usually wear…
  on weekends?
  during the week?
2 What colors do you like for clothes?

7 *KnowHow*: Vocabulary notes

Vocabulary notes are useful. Look at the example.

Write notes about these words.

   clothes   yellow   suit

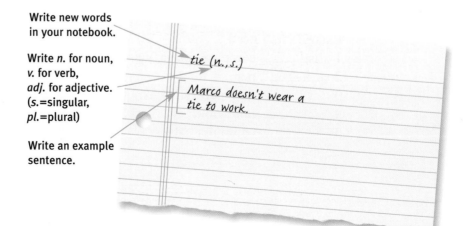

Write new words in your notebook.

Write *n.* for noun, *v.* for verb, *adj.* for adjective. (*s.*=singular, *pl.*=plural)

Write an example sentence.

tie (n., s.)

Marco doesn't wear a tie to work.

8 ▶ In Conversation

AUDIO Complete the conversation. Listen. Then read.

It's $39.50.   They're $8.00 each.

Clerk: Can I help you?
Woman: Yes, please. How much are those hats?
Clerk: ¹_____
Woman: OK, I'll take one. Can I see that
          sweater, please?
Clerk: What size do you need?
Woman: A medium, please. How much is it?
Clerk: ²_____
Woman: Can I try it on?
Clerk: Yes, of course. The fitting room is
          over there.

9 ▶ Focus on Grammar

a Look at the examples. Then practice saying the prices.

$39.50 = thirty-nine dollars and fifty cents OR thirty-nine fifty
$1.75 = one dollar and seventy-five cents OR a dollar seventy-five

$4.30 $65.00 $29.95 $17.40 $58.99

b Look at the chart and fill in the blanks.

How much...? + prices	
Singular	*Plural*
How much **is** this sweater?	How much **are** these hats?
It's $39.50	**They're** $8.00.

1 How much *are* these batteries?
   They're $3.50 for four.
2 How much _____ this camera?
   _____ $95.00.

3 How much _____ those ties?
   _____ $15.99 each.
4 How much _____ that jacket?
   _____ $42.50.

10 ▶ Language in Action: *Can* for requests

Work with a partner. Roleplay a conversation in a store. Ask about items in section 5.

1 Can I help you?	Yes, please. No, thank you. I'm just looking.
2 Can I see (that sweater / those hats)?	Yes, of course.
3 Can I try (it / this / these) on?	Yes, the fitting room is over there.

Example   A: *Hello. Can I help you?*
           B: *Yes. Can I see that T-shirt please?*

11 ▶ Reading

a What do you think? Check one item for each question below.

1 What is the main thing people buy on the Internet?
__ food   __ cars   __ clothes

2 What is one main reason people shop on the Internet?
__ open 24 hours   __ saves time   __ home delivery

b Read the article and check your answers.

HOW POPULAR IS INTERNET SHOPPING?
Recent surveys show that more people use the Internet for shopping these days.

What do Internet shoppers buy?
Many people now buy clothes on the Internet. Clothes are probably the most popular items, but people also buy books, CDs, and computer hardware and software online. Some travelers buy their airline tickets on the Internet, and some people even buy large items like cars. In some places, it is also possible to buy food on the Internet.

Why do people shop on the Internet?
According to many people, there are two main reasons why people shop on the Internet. They say it saves time and that there are no crowds. Also, the Internet is "open" 24 hours a day, and there is often home delivery.

Not everyone likes Internet shopping, though. For example, many people still don't feel comfortable giving out their credit card number over the Internet. There are also many people who actually like to go to stores and shopping malls to buy things!

c How do you like to shop? Check two ways. Compare your answers with other students.

in a shopping mall   __
in a small store   __
in a department store   __
by telephone   __
on the Internet (online)   __

12 ▶ Writing, Listening, and Speaking

a **AUDIO** Look at order form A and listen to the conversation. Which two things are wrong on the order form?

A

T-Shirts Pronto

Shop online www.tshirts.pronto.khw
Order toll free 1-800-555-0000
Customer service 1-800-555-0001
Fax 1-800-555-0002

Name _James Prado_
Address _1466 Westside Drive_
City _Miami_   State _FL_ Zip Code _03466_
Phone (day) _123-555-0219_
Phone (evening) _123-555-6644_
E-mail address _n/a_

Item Number	Description	Color	Size	Quantity	Price
MB1234	Men's T-shirt	black	L	1	$18.95
				TOTAL	$18.95

METHOD OF PAYMENT

☐ Check   ☒ Credit Card

Credit Card Number | 1 | 2 | 3 | 4 | 5 | 6 | 7 | 8 | 9 | 0 | 1 | 2 | 5 | 5 | 5 | 5 |

Expiration Date _11_ (month) / _06_ (year)
Signature _____

T-Shirts Pronto

Women's WB1234   Men's MB1234

Price **$18.95**

Men's MT3567

Women's WT3567   Price **$17.50**

available in sizes S, M, and L
S = small   M = medium   L = large

b Work with a partner. A, choose something from the ad above. B, take A's order and complete order form B. Then reverse roles.

> **Useful questions:**
> Can I take your order?
> What's your name?
> What's your address?
> What's your phone number?
> What's your credit card number?

B

T-Shirts Pronto

Shop online www.tshirts.pronto.khw
Order toll free 1-800-555-0000
Customer service 1-800-555-0001
Fax 1-800-555-0002

Name _____
Address _____
City _____ State _____ Zip Code _____
Phone (day) _____
Phone (evening) _____
E-mail address _____

Item Number	Description	Color	Size	Quantity	Price
				TOTAL	

METHOD OF PAYMENT

☐ Check   ☐ Credit Card

Credit Card Number | | | | | | | | | | | | | | | | |

Expiration Date _____ (month) / _____ (year)
Signature _____

7 Day in, day out!

✔ Everyday activities; showing interest
✔ Simple present: *Wh-* questions; prepositions of time

1 ▶ Vocabulary: Everyday activities

a **AUDIO** Listen and practice these expressions.

get up   start work   eat lunch   finish work   have dinner   go to bed

b What time do you do these things?

2 ▶ In Conversation

AUDIO Which activities happen at different times in Madrid and New York? Listen. Then read.

Kim: So, you're from Madrid. Is it true that daily schedules are different in Madrid and New York?
David: Yes, I think that's true.
Kim: What time do people typically start work?
David: Well, it depends on the job. I work in an office and I start work at 8:30.
Kim: That's typical here, too. Do you eat lunch at noon?
David: No, we don't. We have lunch from 2:00 to 4:00.
Kim: Now, that's different. Most people here have one hour for lunch. And, it's usually from 12:00 to 1:00. What time do you finish work?
David: At 7:00 or 7:30.
Kim: That seems late. When do you have dinner?
David: Oh, usually about 9:30.
Kim: That's really late. I have dinner at 6:30!

39

3 ▶ Focus on Grammar

a Compare the *yes / no* questions and the *Wh-* questions. Find two examples of *Wh-* questions in the conversation on page 39.

Simple present: *Wh-* and *yes / no* questions		
Questions	*Answers*	
Do you **live** in Spain?	Yes, I **do.**	No, I **don't.**
Where **do** you **live**?	In Spain.	
Does he **start** work at 8:30 a.m.?	Yes, he **does.**	No, he **doesn't.**
When **does** he **start** work?	At 8:30 a.m.	

b Match the questions (1–5) and answers (a–e).

1	What does David do?	<u>1d</u>	a	In New York.
2	Where does Kim live?	___	b	At 8:30 a.m.
3	Where does he work?	___	c	Late, after 8:00 p.m.
4	What time does he start work?	___	d	He's a business director.
5	When do people in Spain have dinner?	___	e	In an office.

c Put the words in order to make questions.

Example *get up / you / do / when*
  When do you get up?

1 you / do / what / do

  _____

2 do / live / where / you

  _____

3 start / time / what / you / do / work

  _____

4 lunch / you / have / do / when

  _____

5 do / work / what / you / time / finish

  _____

6 dinner / when / have / do / you

  _____

d Work with a partner. Ask and answer the questions in 3c.

Example   A: *What do you do?*
  B: *I work in a restaurant. I'm a waiter.*

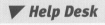

▼ **Help Desk**

What do you do?
means *What is your job?*

4 ▶ Listening

a **AUDIO** Listen to the conversation. Write T (true) or F (false).

1 David talks about hotels in different countries.   —
2 He talks about meal times in hotels.   —
3 He talks about hotel guests from Australia and Japan.   —

b **AUDIO** Listen again and answer the questions.

1 What does David do?
2 Where does he travel?
3 When are the hotel dining rooms open?
4 Who usually eats meals early?

5 ▶ Language in Action: Showing interest

a **AUDIO** Listen. Complete the conversation with expressions from the box.

Kim: What do you do, David?
David: I'm a business director for a hotel company.
Kim: ¹_____ Do you travel a lot?
...
David: What about you Kim? What do you do?
Kim: I'm a marketing manager.
David: ²_____ Where do you work?

> **SHOWING INTEREST**
> • Oh?
> • Really?
> • How interesting!
> • That sounds interesting.

b Complete the conversations with the expressions below.

How interesting! Is he famous?
That sounds interesting. Where do you work?
Really? What's the name of the restaurant?
Oh? Why not?

1 I work in a restaurant.
_____

2 What do you do?
—I'm an architect.
_____

3 I never eat lunch.
_____

4 My brother is an actor.
_____

c Work with a partner. Practice the conversations from 5b. Try to include real information.

6 ▶ Reading

a Can you put the words and phrases into the appropriate category?

a hospital   an editor   patients   write an article
pick up a package   deliver a baby   deliver a package interview

Doctor	Journalist	Package courier
a hospital		

b Read the paragraphs. Write the jobs below the names.

Everyday Living

Kathryn Flory, _____

Mindy Dodge, _____

Kathryn Flory works from Monday to Thursday and some weekends. She is "on call" one day a week. On that day, the hospital calls her day or night when there is a problem or to deliver a baby. She has breakfast with her family and helps her two daughters get ready for school. She starts work at 8:30 a.m. She sees patients and sometimes goes to the hospital during the day. She gets home at 6:30 p.m. Her husband makes dinner. After dinner, she relaxes with her family.

Mindy Dodge gets up at 6:00 a.m. during the week. She does some exercise and then she goes to work. She has breakfast at work. She doesn't take a lunch break. She eats lunch at her desk. She interviews people and writes articles for most of the day. She talks to her editor and finishes her stories at the end of the day. She reads or watches TV in the evening. She goes to bed at 11:00 p.m.

Thomas Powers gets up at 5:45 in the morning and has breakfast at 6:15. He starts work at 7:00 a.m. He delivers packages for most of the morning. He has lunch from 12:15 to 2:00 p.m. He walks about 12 miles in a day and stops at about 90 offices. He picks up or delivers about 250–300 packages in a day. He finishes work at 6:00 p.m.

Thomas Powers, _____

c Read the paragraphs again. Answer the questions.

1 Who gets up before 6:00 a.m.?   *Thomas Powers* _____
2 Who eats breakfast and lunch at work?   _____
3 Who does exercise before work?   _____
4 Who is "on call" one day a week?   _____
5 Who walks a lot at work?   _____
6 Who has children?   _____
7 Who reads or watches TV in the evening? _____

KnowHow: Linking with s

a **AUDIO** Listen to these sentences. Notice how some words are linked with *s*.

He walks a lot.
He gets up at 7:00 a.m.
She does exercise before work.
She works at night.

b **AUDIO** Listen again and practice saying the sentences.

Focus on Grammar

a Look at the sentences in the chart. Then find an example of each preposition in 6b.

Prepositions of time: *In, on, at, from...to, during*		
Time	*Parts of the day*	*Days, week, and weekend*
He gets up **at** 7:00 a.m.	She works...	He gets up early...
She works **from** 8 **to** 5.	**in** the morning.	**on** Mondays.
	in the afternoon.	**on** weekends.
	in the evening.	**on** Sunday morning.
	at night.	**during** the week.

b Make sentences about Mark.

Mark Blake—chef

> **▼ Help Desk**
>
> Add *-s* to days of the week and *weekend* to show that something is a routine.
>
> *on Tuesday***s** = every Tuesday
>
> *on weekend***s** = every weekend

Example   work–afternoon, night   *He works in the afternoon and at night.*

1   not work—Mondays, Tuesdays
2   start work—4:00 p.m.
3   finish work—11:30 p.m.
4   have dinner—12:00 a.m.
5   go to bed—2:00 a.m.
6   get up—9:00 a.m.
7   have breakfast—10:00 a.m.–10:30 a.m.

c Now make six sentences about yourself. Use the expressions above.

Examples *I don't work on weekends. I watch TV in the evening.*

d Work in small groups and compare your routines and activities. Find two things that are similar and two that are different.

9 ▶ Speaking and Writing

7 a.m.—morning

10 p.m.—night

a Read the paragraphs. Which person is a morning person? A night person? How do you know?

Julia

> I'm always tired in the morning, and I don't like to get up early. I go to bed at 1:00 or 2:00 a.m. because I always do a lot in the evening and at night. I love weekends. I get up late, at 10:00 or 11:00 a.m., and I go to bed when I want.

Steve

> I get up at 5:30 or 6:00 a.m. every day, even on weekends. I have a lot of energy in the morning. I go to bed at 9:30 or 10:00 every night. My friends think I'm crazy, but that's OK. I do a lot while they sleep!

b Work with a partner. Use these questions (or your own) and interview your partner.

What time do you get up during the week?   On weekends?
What time do you go to bed during the week?   On weekends?
What time of day do you have a lot of energy?   Do you like mornings?

c Write a paragraph about your partner. Explain why you think he or she is a morning person or a night person (or in between).

d Work as a class. How many people are in each category?

Number	Total
morning person	
night person	
in between	

8 Essential ingredients

✔ Food; offering, accepting, and refusing
✔ Countable and uncountable nouns; *some* and *any*

1 ▸ Vocabulary: Food

a Read the menu for The Salad Spot.

The Salad Spot

SALAD BAR	SANDWICHES	SOUP of the day/DRINKS
Lettuce		Vegetable soup
Broccoli	**Sandwich meats**	
Olives	Chicken	Tea
Green Peppers	Roast beef	Coffee
Onions		Soda

b **AUDIO** Listen. Some of the foods below are also on The Salad Spot menu. Check the items you hear.

___ carrots ___ potatoes ___ tomatoes ___ lemons ___ strawberries

___ bananas ___ oranges ___ rice ___ bread ___ cheese

c **AUDIO** Work with a partner. Practice reading the menu aloud. Then listen and check your pronunciation.

d Discuss the questions.

1   Are salad bars typical in restaurants in your area?
2   What do you like in a salad? What don't you like?

2 In Conversation

AUDIO What does Rob want to eat? Listen. Then read.

Lucy: What a great salad bar! Hey, your salad is so small.

Rob: It's OK. I have lettuce and tomatoes.

Lucy: That's all? You don't have broccoli or olives or onions or even dressing. That's not a salad!

Rob: Don't worry. I'm not finished. I want soup and a sandwich after this!

3 Focus on Grammar

a Look at the chart. Circle the correct word in each sentence.

1 Use *a* or *an* with (countable / uncountable) nouns in the singular.
2 (Countable / uncountable) nouns are not usually plural.

Countable and uncountable nouns	
Countable nouns	**Uncountable nouns**
Rob wants **a sandwich**.	Rob wants **soup** after his salad.
He likes **sandwiches**.	He likes **soup**.

b Look at these words from the conversation. Then add the other food words from page 45 to the lists.

Countable nouns	Uncountable nouns
a sandwich / sandwiches	soup
a tomato / tomatoes	lettuce
an olive / olives	broccoli
an onion / onions	dressing

▼ **Help Desk**

It is possible to "count" uncountable nouns.

I drink coffee. (uncountable)

*I drink **two cups of** coffee every morning.* (You can count cups.)

c Make true sentences. Then compare your answers with a partner.

1 I like….
2 I don't like….
3 I eat…every day.
4 I drink…every day.

Examples *I like potatoes and tomatoes. I don't like cheese. I eat a sandwich every day.*

4 ▶ In Conversation

AUDIO What food does Kay ask about that's <u>not</u> for the soup? Listen. Then read.

Kay: Hi, Alex. I'm at the store, and I don't have the shopping list. What do we need?

Alex: Well, I'm making vegetable soup for dinner, so let's see… We need some carrots.

Kay: OK. What else?

Alex: Hmm. Ah, yes. We need some onions and some garlic, too. Oh, we don't have any potatoes. Some potatoes…and I think that's everything.

Kay: OK,…uh…do we have any chocolate?

Alex: Chocolate? I don't need any chocolate for soup.

Kay: I know, but I love chocolate!

5 ▶ Focus on Grammar

a Look at the chart. Find two examples of *some* and *any* in section 4.

Some and Any		
Affirmative statements	**Negative statements**	**Questions**
We need **some** carrots.	We don't have **any** potatoes.	Do we have **any** chocolate?

b Fill in the blanks with *some* or *any*.

1 Do we have ___*any*___ rice?
2 We need _____ beef for dinner.
3 I don't have _____ apples. Do you like bananas?
4 Do you have _____ milk?
5 Please buy _____ potatoes.
6 They don't have _____ strawberries at the supermarket.

c Look at the picture and make sentences. Use *some* or *any*.

Examples *They have some garlic.*
They don't have any onions.
They need some tea.

6 KnowHow: Grammar notes

a It's helpful to make your own notes about new grammar. Look at this example.

1. Organize information.

2. Underline important points.

3. Write an example sentence.

(+) statements	(-) statements	(?) questions
Use some	Use any	Use any
I eat some fruit every day.	We don't have any coffee at home.	Do you have any milk?

b Make similar notes about countable and uncountable nouns from 3b on page 46.

7 Listening

AUDIO Listen to the conversation. What are the two special ingredients in the soup? Does Kay like the soup?

cinnamon and other spices

hot chile peppers

fish / seafood

8 Language in Action: Polite offers

a **AUDIO** Listen. Which conversation do you hear?

1
Would you like more pie?
—Yes, please. It's very good.

2
Would you like more pie?
—No, thank you. It's very good, but I'm full.

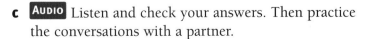

b Match the offers (1–4) and responses (a–d).

1 Would you like a piece of cake? _1d_   a No, thank you. I don't drink tea.
2 Would you like a sandwich? __   b No, thank you. I'm not hungry.
3 Would you like a cup of coffee? __   c Yes, please. Coffee sounds good.
4 Would you like a cup of tea? __   d No, thanks. I'm on a diet.

c **AUDIO** Listen and check your answers. Then practice the conversations with a partner.

> ▼ **Help Desk**
>
> People usually give a reason or explanation when they refuse an offer.
>
> *I don't drink tea. / I'm on a diet.*

48

9 Reading

a Look at the map. Which ingredients do you think are popular in these areas of the United States?

a lot of spices   fish   beans
fresh fruit   chile peppers   rice

b Read the article and check your answers.

Do you think food in the United States is only hamburgers and hot dogs? This week we look at cooking in different parts of the country. Read our article to see how interesting and varied it really is!

California

There are many different influences in California cooking, but most important are Chinese, Japanese, and Mexican. The many fresh ingredients –fruits, vegetables, fish, and

The South

Many influences make up the rich flavors of Southern cooking: Native American, British, French, and Spanish. Most famous though, are the vegetables, spices, and ways of cooking that came with slaves from Africa. "Gumbo" is one well-known example. There are many different recipes for gumbo, but shrimp, sausage, tomatoes, onions, a lot of spices, and rice are usually in this delicious dish.

other kinds of seafood– are also important. California is especially famous for its avocados and fresh salads. One recipe combines avocados with tomatoes, snow peas, and mushrooms to make a beautiful and delicious salad.

The Southwest

People think of bright colors and spicy flavors when they think of Southwestern food. Native American, Mexican, and Spanish traditions are all part of this popular cooking. Meat, rice, and beans with flavorful sauces are typical, but chile peppers are the most important ingredient. They make this cooking different. For example, a simple vegetable soup with Southwestern ingredients becomes special. It has vegetables and beans, and also two kinds of chile peppers.

c Read the article again. Complete the chart.

International Influences in American Cooking

	The South	California	The Southwest
African	✓		
Native American	✓		
British	✓		
Chinese			
French	✓		
Japanese			
Mexican			
Spanish	✓		

d Which type of cooking do you think you would like?

10 Speaking

a Work in small groups and discuss these questions.

1 In general, do people eat more meat or fish in your country?
2 What are the most popular vegetables?
3 What are the most popular kinds of fruit?
4 What do people typically drink with meals?
5 Are there differences in food in different areas of your country? Give examples.

b Compare answers. Do different groups have similar answers or not?

11 Writing

a Imagine that you are writing a paragraph in a magazine about food in your country. Make some notes from your answers in 10a, then write your paragraph.

b Read another student's paragraph. Do you think it gives a clear idea of food in your country?

Grammar

Ritzy Hotel
Name(s): Takeshi and Kumiko Sato
Nationality: Japanese

Hi, I'm Jason. I live in New York and I work at the front desk in a famous hotel. I use a telephone and a computer at work. Our guests come from many different countries. I speak English and Spanish, and I study Japanese. I work at night, from 10 p.m. to 6 a.m. I go home at 6:15. At home, I eat breakfast and read the morning newspaper. After breakfast, I go to bed. On weekends, I spend time with my wife and children.

1 Complete the questions and short answers. Then write the correct information.

1 _Does_ Jason work during the day?
No, he _doesn't_ .
He works at night.

2 _____ Jason single?
No, he _____ .
_____

3 _____ all the hotel guests come from the United States?
No, they _____ .
_____

4 _____ Takeshi and Kumiko Sato from Canada?
No, they _____ .
_____

5 _____ Jason eat breakfast at the hotel?
No, he _____ .
_____

2 Complete the paragraph with the correct prepositions.

in on at from to

Jason goes to Japanese class ¹_on_ Monday. He works ²_____ night, so he goes to class ³_____ the morning. His class is ⁴_____ 9:00 ⁵_____ 10:30. He doesn't work ⁶_____ weekends, so he is not tired ⁷_____ Monday mornings.

3 Write the questions for these answers. The words in **bold** are the answers.

1 What _____?
Takeshi Sato is a **businessman**.

2 _____?
He and his wife live **in Tokyo**.

3 _____?
They come to New York **in October**.

4 _____?
She (Kumiko) usually eats breakfast **at 7:30**.

4 Complete the sentences with true information about yourself.

1 I'm a _____ .
2 I work (study) at _____ .
_____ .
3 I get up at _____ .
4 For lunch I eat _____ .
_____ .
5 On Saturday afternoons, I _____ .
_____ .

5 Now complete the same information about a classmate.

1 _____ is a _____ .
(Classmate's name)
2 He (she) works _____ .
3 _____
4 _____
5 _____

6 ▶ Complete the conversation with *this*, *that*, *these*, *those*, or *How much*.

Takeshi: Oh, look at ¹ _these_ hats.
Kumiko: ² _____ are they?
Takeshi: They're $65 each! How much are ³ _____ sunglasses?
Kumiko: They're $90! And ⁴ _____ shirt is $135!
Takeshi: Look, ⁵ _____ coffee mug is only $5. Let's buy two!

7 ▶ Complete the conversation with *some* or *any*.

Waiter: Would you like the soup or a salad?
Takeshi: I'd like ¹ _some_ vegetable soup, please. And do you have ² _____ bread?
Waiter: Yes we do. And you, Ma'am?
Kumiko: I'd like the Greek salad with ³ _____ black olives, but I don't want ⁴ _____ onions.
Takeshi: Do you have ⁵ _____ green tea?
Waiter: I'm sorry, we don't have ⁶ _____ green tea. Would you like ⁷ _____ black tea?
Takeshi: No, thank you.

Vocabulary

8 ▶ Underline the different word in each group. Then write the topic of each group in the space.

clothes   family   colors   food

1 _colors_ : red   orange   <u>sweater</u>   white
2 _____ : cable   soup   rice   sandwich
3 _____ : boots   shirt   actor   T-shirt
4 _____ : niece   cousin   bicycle   father

Add three more words to each group.

Recycling Center

Ritzy Hotel

Name(s): _Takeshi and Kumiko Sato_
Nationality: _Japanese_
Address: _86921 Bessho, Tokyo_
Telephone: _3459-6481_
E-mail: _tksato@web.khw_

9 ▶ Read the registration form. Write the questions Jason asked Mr. and Mrs. Sato.

1 _What's your name?_ _____
2 _____
3 _____
4 _____
5 _____

Fun Spot

A riddle is a funny or "trick" question. Can you answer this riddle?

Don has a photograph of someone. His friend asks, "Who is it?" Don says, "That man's father is my father's son." (Don has no brothers.)

Who is in the photograph?

Can you find the answer? If not, arrange these letters into two words.   ONOSSND

9 In the neighborhood

✔ Places; neighborhoods; asking about location
✔ *There is / are*; prepositions of place

1 ▶ Reading

a Read the postcard. Which place in the picture is mentioned?
Find a place in the picture that is <u>not</u> mentioned.

Dear Melanie,

Hi! I'm in a beautiful little town, and it's very interesting. There's a restaurant next to the hotel, and there are some beautiful parks near here, too. There isn't a lot of traffic, so it's very quiet. It's a really nice neighborhood!

—Jay

Melanie Williams

2398 Powell Boulevard

Evanston, Illinois

b What do you think? Would you like to visit this place?

2 ▶ Vocabulary: Names for places

a Look at the map key. Fill in the blanks with the places on the list.

bank   bus stop   post office   bookstore

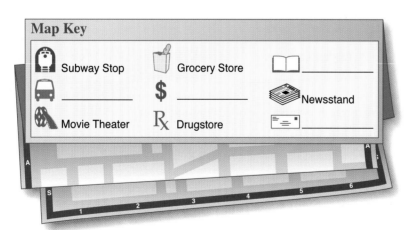

Map Key

Subway Stop   Grocery Store   _____
_____ $ _____   Newsstand
Movie Theater   Rx Drugstore   _____

b **AUDIO** Listen and check your answers. Then practice saying the words.

3 ▶ Focus on Grammar

a Look at the chart. Find three examples of *There is / are* in the postcard on page 53.

There is / are	
Singular	*Plural*
There is a bookstore in the neighborhood. **There isn't** a bookstore in the neighborhood.	**There are** a lot of stores in the neighborhood. **There aren't** a lot of stores in the neighborhood.
Is there a bookstore in the neighborhood? Yes, **there is.** No, **there isn't.**	**Are there** a lot of stores in the neighborhood? Yes, **there are.** No, **there aren't.**
Note: Contractions with *there* There's = There is There is no contraction for *there are*.	

b Complete the sentences with *there's* or *there are*. Use the negative form when indicated.

¹ __There's__ a bus stop, but ² _____ (not) a subway stop in my neighborhood.
³ _____ some restaurants and stores.
⁴ _____ a little grocery store on the corner.
⁵ _____ two banks, but ⁶ _____ (not) a post office. It's a little noisy, but I like it.

This neighborhood is very quiet. ⁷ _____ a grocery store and ⁸ _____ a drugstore, but ⁹ _____ (not) a lot of other stores. We go to a different town for shopping. ¹⁰ _____ a restaurant and a café. ¹¹ _____ (not) a movie theater, but ¹² _____ a video store. That's good!

c Work in small groups. Think of the area where you study and make sentences. Then compare your answers.

  1 Make five sentences using *there is / are*.
  2 Make five sentences using *there isn't / aren't*.

4 ▶ In Conversation

AUDIO What are they looking for? How are they going to get there? Listen. Then read.

Jill: So, where's the Convention Center?
Luc: I'm not quite sure. I think it's near the harbor.
Jill: Do we have a map?
Luc: I have this drawing…. It's not exactly a map.
Jill: Let's see…it looks like the Convention Center is on Central Avenue, next to the National Theater.
Luc: Yes, that looks right. OK, let's go. There's a subway stop across the street.
Jill: Let's take a taxi. It's faster.
Luc: Good idea! Then we don't need the map.

5 ▶ Focus on Grammar

a Look at the chart. Find four examples of the prepositions in the conversation above.

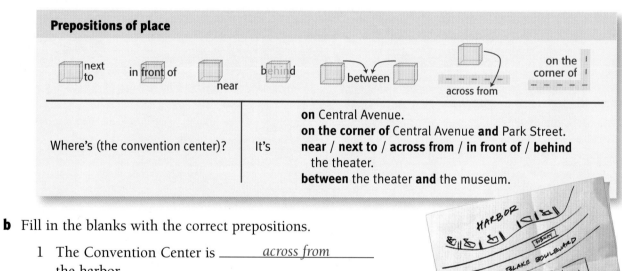

Prepositions of place

next to	in front of	near	behind	between	across from	on the corner of

Where's (the convention center)?	It's	**on** Central Avenue. **on the corner of** Central Avenue **and** Park Street. **near / next to / across from / in front of / behind** the theater. **between** the theater **and** the museum.

b Fill in the blanks with the correct prepositions.

1 The Convention Center is _____*across from*_____ the harbor.
2 The National Theater is _____ Central Avenue _____ Blake Boulevard.
3 The Harbor Hotel is _____ the Convention Center.
4 The Convention Center is _____ the Harbor Hotel _____ the National Theater.
5 There's a parking lot _____ the Convention Center.

c Work with a partner. Make five questions about places in your town or city. Then ask other students your questions.

Example   A: *Where's the Riverview Shopping Center?*
             B: *It's on Grand Avenue, next to the…*

▼ Help Desk

Be careful:

*It's **near** the museum.*
(Not: ~~It's near to the museum.~~)

BUT

*It's **next to** the museum.*
(Not: ~~It's next the museum.~~)

KnowHow: Listening tips

a Think about listening to an English tape or CD in class. How do you feel about it?

> **I like it.**   **It's OK.**   **It's difficult.**

b Look at the suggestions below. Then do the listening activity in section 7.

1 Think about the topic before you listen.
2 Listen for the general idea first.
3 Don't worry if you don't understand every word. Use key words to help you understand.
4 Listen more than once.

7 Listening

a Before you listen, discuss the two maps.

> Example   *The Star Café is between the bank and Devon Market.*

b 🔊 **AUDIO** Listen and answer the questions.

1 How does Tim feel about the neighborhood?
2 Which places does he talk about?

c 🔊 **AUDIO** Listen again. Which map is described?

Language in Action: Places

a Practice the conversation.

> A: Excuse me. Is there a grocery store near here?
> B: Yes, there is. Devon Market. It's on Gold Street, next to the café.
> A: OK, thank you.
> B: You're welcome.

ASKING ABOUT PLACES	ANSWERING
Excuse me, is there a grocery store near here?	Yes, there is. It's… No, there isn't. I'm sorry, I don't know.

b Work with a partner. **A**, you are a tourist. Ask about a place. **B**, describe the location.

9 ▶ Reading

a Look at the two town plans. Which do you like? Give reasons for your answer.

b Read the article. Which town plan do the "new urbanists" use?

New Urbanism

There's a new approach to town and city planning in the United States these days.

Currently, many people live in suburbs, large residential areas outside major cities. In these areas stores, schools, and work places are often far away from people's homes. These communities sometimes have no center. Cars are a necessity. Parents drive their children to school, and they drive to the stores. People don't walk very much. They don't see or talk to their neighbors on the street.

Now some town planners and architects are designing small, integrated towns, where it's possible to walk almost anywhere. Their ideas are called New Urbanism. There are now 300–500 New Urbanism projects planned or being built in the United States. One example is Vermillion, a new neighborhood in Huntersville, North Carolina.

These are some of the principles of New Urbanism:

- There is a clear center to the neighborhood. This is often a square or a plaza.
- Most houses or apartments are within a five-minute walk of the center.
- There are different kinds of houses and apartments, with varying prices.
- There is a variety of stores and offices in the neighborhood.
- It's possible for children to walk to the elementary school.
- There are narrow streets with trees along them. This slows traffic and makes it better for people who walk or ride bicycles.

c Check the sentences that describe communities based on New Urbanism.

___ 1 You often see people riding bikes or walking.
___ 2 Children go to school by car or bus.
___ 3 People don't usually walk to work.
___ 4 There's a central area with stores and other public places.
___ 5 All the houses are the same.
___ 6 You don't need a car all the time.

10 ▶ Speaking

a Discuss these questions.

1 Where do you walk in your community? To school? To the supermarket? To work?
2 Where do you drive or go by bus or other transportation?
3 Do you know the people in your neighborhood?
4 What do you think of the New Urbanism principles?

b Work with a partner. Design an "ideal neighborhood." Choose eight locations and place them on the map below. Use these ideas (or your own):

bank	post office	café	restaurant
newsstand	movie theater	school	grocery store
museum	drugstore	hospital	bookstore

c Describe your neighborhood to another pair.

11 ▶ Writing

a Imagine a brochure advertising houses in your "ideal neighborhood." Use your plan from 10b and write a paragraph describing the area.

b Read about other students' neighborhoods. Which do you like best? Why?

A Nice Place to Live!

This is a very special neighborhood.

It has everything you need.
There's a bank and a post office.
There's a grocery store...

10 Fun and games

✔ Sports, games, and abilities
✔ *Can / can't* (ability); conjunctions

 Vocabulary: Sports

a Work with a partner. Do the quiz.

How much do you know about popular sports around the world?
Take our quiz and find out!

Which sport do you think is the most popular in each country?

1. Canada   a. baseball
2. Germany   b. basketball
3. Japan   c. golf
4. Norway   d. ice hockey
5. The Philippines   e. skiing
6. Scotland   f. soccer

What is the most popular sport in the world?

a. golf   b. soccer   c. baseball

Golf

Basketball

Skiing

Ice Hockey

Soccer

Baseball

b **AUDIO** Listen and check your answers.

c Discuss the questions.

1 Which sports are popular or not popular where you live?
2 Which sports do you like or not like?

Examples   *Soccer is very popular. Ice hockey isn't popular.*
                I like soccer and basketball. I don't like golf.
                I don't like any sports!

2 ▶ Reading

Match each sentence (a–d) with the correct picture.

a They can skate as fast as 60 km an hour.
b They can ride at an average of 40–50 km an hour.
c They can't run at maximum speed for four hours after a race.
d Professionals can lift up to 25 tons in one training session.

Amazing Athletes

100-meter sprinters
¹ *Elite sprinters can run up to 40 km an hour.*
2 _____

Downhill mountain bikers
3 _____
⁴ *They can't stop easily.*

Weightlifters
5 _____

Speed skaters
6 _____

3 ▶ Focus on Grammar

a Look at the sentences in the chart. Does the main verb, *run*, change after *can*?

Can (ability)	
Affirmative statements	**Negative statements**
I You He / She / It **can** run fast. We They	I You He / She / It **can't (cannot)** run fast. We They
Questions	**Answers**
Can you run fast?	**Yes, I can.** **No, I can't.**

b Circle C (correct) or I (incorrect). Rewrite the incorrect sentences.

1 A sprinter can ~~to~~ run fast.   C Ⓘ   *A sprinter can run fast.*
2 He can't lift it.   C I   _____
3 A speed skater not can stop easily.   C I   _____
4 Do you can skate?   C I   _____
5 Can mountain bikers ride fast?   C I   _____

c Write five true sentences about yourself. Then compare answers with a partner.

Examples *I can run fast. I can't kick a ball far.*

4 ▸ *KnowHow*: Pronunciation of *can* and *can't*

a **AUDIO** Listen to the pronunciation of *can* and *can't* in these sentences.

I can run a kilometer.	/kən/	Can you skate?	/kən/
I can't run fast.	/kænt/	Yes, I can.	/kæn/
		No, I can't.	/kænt/

Now practice the sentences with a partner.

b **AUDIO** Listen. Check the sentence you hear.

1 He can ride a bicycle. — He can't ride a bicycle. —
2 I can ski. — I can't ski. —
3 They can ice skate. — They can't ice skate. —

c Practice saying your sentences from 3c.

5 ▸ Speaking

a Think of a sport. Make four sentences about what good athletes *can* do. Use the ideas below or your own ideas.

run   jump   throw   hit   kick

basketball players   baseball players   golfers   soccer players   volleyball players

run fast   jump high   throw a ball far   kick a ball far   hit a ball far

Example *Good basketball players can jump high.*

b Describe the athletes. Can other students guess the sport?

Example A: *They can jump high.*
          B: *They play basketball.*

61

6 ⟩ Reading

a Can you find these activities in the illustration below?

cook   make jewelry   draw and paint   play the trumpet   play the drums

b Read the article. Why is Richie so interesting?

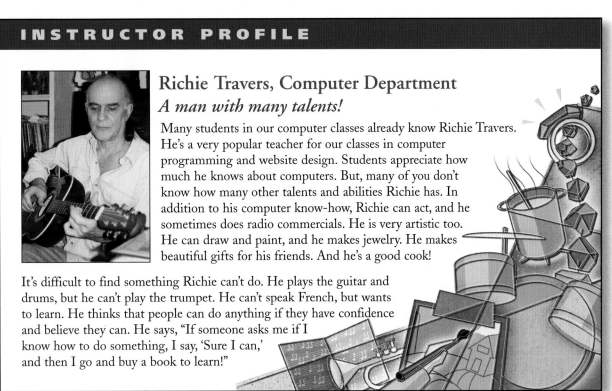

INSTRUCTOR PROFILE

Richie Travers, Computer Department
A man with many talents!

Many students in our computer classes already know Richie Travers. He's a very popular teacher for our classes in computer programming and website design. Students appreciate how much he knows about computers. But, many of you don't know how many other talents and abilities Richie has. In addition to his computer know-how, Richie can act, and he sometimes does radio commercials. He is very artistic too. He can draw and paint, and he makes jewelry. He makes beautiful gifts for his friends. And he's a good cook!

It's difficult to find something Richie can't do. He plays the guitar and drums, but he can't play the trumpet. He can't speak French, but wants to learn. He thinks that people can do anything if they have confidence and believe they can. He says, "If someone asks me if I know how to do something, I say, 'Sure I can,' and then I go and buy a book to learn!"

c Read the article again. Complete the chart.

	He can...	He can't...	He can't..., but wants to learn.
design a website	✓		
play the trumpet			
make jewelry			
speak French			
act			
draw and paint			

d Do you know someone with a lot of talents and abilities? What can he / she do? What can't he / she do?

> ▼ **Help Desk**
>
> Use *play* with games and musical instruments.
>
> *She **plays** soccer.*
>
> *He **plays** the guitar.*
>
> Don't use *the* with the name of the sport.

7 ▶ Focus on Grammar

a Look at the chart. Complete the sentences.

1 Use _or_ for alternatives.
2 Use _____ for contrasting ideas.
3 Use _____ for similar or related ideas.

Conjunctions: *and, but, or*

I can draw **and** paint.
He acts, **but** he can't sing.
She wants to learn how to play the guitar **or** the drums.

Note: He can't sing **or** dance. = He can't sing, **and** he can't dance.

---

b Fill in the blanks.

1 I like sports, _but_ I don't like basketball.
2 I love music. I can play the guitar _____ the piano.
3 What do you want to play now, volleyball _____ tennis?
4 I don't have many hobbies, _____ I like photography.
5 Can you study Japanese _____ Spanish
   at the same time?
6 I can't paint _____ draw.
7 I can't ride a bike, _____ I would like to learn.

8 ▶ Language in Action: Offering help

a **AUDIO** Listen. Complete the conversation with the
expressions Diane and Tim use.

OFFERING	ACCEPTING	REFUSING
I can teach you.	OK!	Thanks, but I don't
I can show you.	Thanks!	have time.
I'll teach you.	That'd be great.	No, thanks.
I'll show you.		

Diane: Do you want to play golf today?
Tim: Sorry, I don't know how to play golf.
Diane: That's OK. [1]_____.
Tim: Really? [2]_____.

b Work with a partner. Practice the conversation.
Use different activities and expressions.
Find something that your partner can teach you!

▼ Help Desk

I don't know how to is similar
to *I can't*.

I don't know how to is better in
the conversation between Diane
and Tim. It means that Tim never
learned to play golf.

---

9 Listening

a **AUDIO** Read the game show questions. Listen and mark the questions they *don't* use.

XYZ TV   How Much Do You Know ?

Contestant Questions: Circle Y (Yes) or N (No) for each question.

	Y	N
1. Can he/she cook?	Y	N
2. Can he/she sing?	Y	N
3. Can he/she fix cars?	Y	N
4. Does he/she like TV?	Y	N
5. Does he/she like sports?	Y	N
6. Can he/she swim?	Y	N
7. Can he/she ice skate?	Y	N

b **AUDIO** Listen again. Write the answers to the questions you hear.

c Think of someone you know well. Can you answer questions 1–7 about him / her?

10 Writing

a Read Louis's description of himself for the TV game show. What does he say for each category?

—athletic
—artistic or creative
—mechanical

b Write notes about yourself for each category (athletic, artistic or creative, mechanical). Then, write a paragraph.

XYZ TV   How Much Do You Know?

Name: _____

1. Write a short description of things you can and can't do.
_____
_____
_____

XYZ TV   How Much Do You Know?

Name: _Louis Rivers_

1. Write a short description of things you can and can't do.

I'm very athletic. I love most sports.
I play soccer, basketball, and volleyball
very well. I can swim but I can't ice
skate. I'm not very artistic or creative.
I can't draw or paint. I can sing a
little, but I don't play an instrument.
I like photography and I take a lot
of pictures. I'm not very mechanical;
I love cars and motorcycles, but I
can't fix them.

2. Why do you want to be a contestant on "How Much

c Read another student's paragraph. Does it give enough information for the TV game show?

11 Home phone

✔ Rooms in a house; telephone language
✔ Present continuous: Statements and questions

 **Reading**

Read the comments about telephones. Which person's phone use is similar to yours?

1

Karen Wong
Seattle, Washington, United States:
I use the phone a lot. I have a phone in my bedroom at home, and I carry a cell phone. I talk to my friends a lot on the phone, and I use the phone to make arrangements with them.

2

Martial and Sylvie Legrand
Evian, France:
We have a phone in the kitchen that everyone in the family uses. We use the phone to make arrangements and things like that, but we don't talk for hours on the phone.

3

Miguel Tavares
Santiago, Dominican Republic:
I use the phone all the time for work. I'm probably on the phone for several hours every day. I have a cell phone, and there's a regular phone in every room of my house...except the bathroom!

2 Vocabulary: Rooms in a house

a **AUDIO** Listen and practice. Who does this house belong to? Write the number of the photo from section 1. ___

b Where are the phones? Name the rooms.

Example   *There's a phone in the living room. There isn't a phone in the garage.*

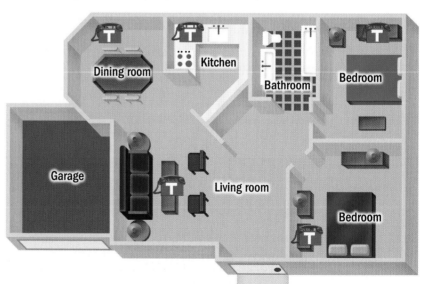

3 Listening

AUDIO Which activities does Jim mention? Listen. Then read.

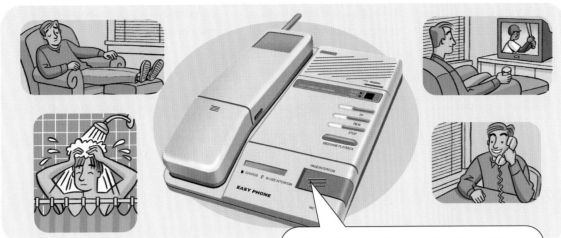

> Hi, this is Jim. I can't come to the phone right now. I'm probably working...or I'm sleeping...or maybe I'm taking a shower...I'm not talking on the phone, though! Anyway, leave a message. Thanks!

4 Focus on Grammar

a Look at the chart. Answer the questions about the following sentences.

*Jim's **taking** a shower.   Jim **takes** a shower every morning.*

1   Which sentence is in the present continuous?
2   Which sentence talks about something that happens every day?

Present continuous: Statements			
I'm		I'm **not**	
You**'re**		You **aren't**	
He / She / It**'s**	**sleeping.**	He / She / It **isn't**	**sleeping.**
We**'re**		We **aren't**	
They**'re**		They **aren't**	

b Look at the chart above. Then complete the e-mail.

E-mail
From: suzieq@eln.khw
To: maggs@wol.khw
Subject: Quiet Friday

Hi, Maggie!

    Finally, it's Friday! I *'m relaxing* _____ ¹(*relax*) this evening. Martial's in the kitchen. He _____ ²(*not work*) tonight (for once!), so he _____ ³(*cook*) dinner. The kids are in the living room. I'm not sure what they _____ ⁴(*do*)...but it's quiet.

    What about you? I'm sure you _____ ⁵(*do*) something exciting tonight. You're probably _____ ⁶(*dance*) in a club or something like that right now...

66

5 ▶ Speaking

a ▶ **AUDIO** Listen. Discuss what the people are doing.

playing basketball	talking on the telephone	cooking	sleeping
taking a shower	using a computer	watching TV	

Example   A: *I think he's cooking.*
         B: *No, I think he's using a computer.*

b Work with a partner. Think of three people you know. Say what each person probably is or isn't doing right now.

Example   *My boyfriend isn't working right now. He's probably driving home.*

6 ▶ *KnowHow*: Spelling *-ing* forms

a Spelling in English can be difficult, but sometimes there are patterns. Look at these examples of one-syllable verbs. Answer the questions.

take—taking	sit—sitting	talk—talking
use—using	run—running	sleep—sleeping

What happens when you add *-ing*…

1 to words that end in a consonant + *e*?
2 to one-syllable words that end in one vowel + one consonant?

b Write the *-ing* form of these words.

   drive   get   eat   dance   put   have

7 ▶ Listening

a ▶ **AUDIO** Listen to the four phone calls. Who can talk on the phone right now? Check the name.

   1 Peter   __
   2 Daniela   __
   3 Miriam   __
   4 Steve   __

b ▶ **AUDIO** Listen again. What is each person doing?

8 In Conversation

AUDIO Does Mark know what his neighbor is doing? Listen. Then read.

Timothy: What is your neighbor doing?
Mark: I don't know.
Timothy: Is he moving furniture or something?
Mark: Maybe. I'm not sure.
Timothy: Does it bother you?
Mark: Not really. He does it a lot.
Patricia: Hey, I hope he isn't getting ready for a party.
Mark: Why?
Patricia: Because we aren't invited!

9 Focus on Grammar

a Look at the chart. Find examples of *Wh-* and *yes / no* questions in section 8.

Present continuous: Questions	
Questions	*Answers*
What **are** they **doing**?	They**'re moving** furniture.
Are they **moving** furniture?	Yes, they **are.** No, they **aren't.**
What**'s** she **doing**?	She**'s moving** furniture.
Is she **moving** furniture?	Yes, she **is.** No, she **isn't.**

b Match the questions (1–6) and answers (a–f).

1 What are you doing?   *1c*   a They're playing basketball.
2 Is she talking on the phone? ___   b No, I'm listening to the radio.
3 Where is Marta sleeping? ___   c I'm cooking dinner.
4 What's he reading? ___   d No, she isn't.
5 What are they doing? ___   e A magazine.
6 Are you watching TV? ___   f In her bedroom.

c **AUDIO** Listen and check your answers. Then practice asking the questions.

d Write questions.

1 What / he / do   *What's he doing?*
2 she / watch / TV   *Is she watching TV?*
3 they / eat / dinner   _____
4 Where / they / sit   _____
5 he / talk / on the telephone   _____
6 she / use / the computer   _____

68

10 Speaking

a Work with a partner. **A**, look at picture 1 for one minute. Then cover the picture. **B**, ask questions about the picture. Use the questions below and add your own ideas.

What's the man / woman doing?

What's the man / woman wearing?

Are the women in the living room?

Are the women sitting or standing?

b Now change roles. **B**, look at picture 2 for one minute. **A**, ask questions about the picture.

11 Language in Action: Telephone language

a Try to complete the conversations with expressions from the chart.

CALLER	PERSON ANSWERING
This is (name).	Hello.
Is (name) there?	Yes, he / she is. OR No, he / she isn't.
Can I speak to (name), please?	Who's calling, please?
	Just a minute.
	One moment, please.

CALL 1

    A: Hello.
    B: Hi, this is Katrina. [1]_____*Is*_____
       Ray _____?
    A: No, [2]_____. He's playing golf.
    B: OK, I'll call back later.

CALL 2

    C: Good morning, Block Company.
    D: [3]_____
       Ms. Galli, please?
    C: [4]_____?
    D: This is Mike Boas.
    C: [5]_____.

b **AUDIO** Now listen and check your answers.

c Work with a partner. Practice the conversations. Use your own names (and different activities if the person isn't there).

12 ▶ Reading and Writing

a Look at the pictures. Describe the scene. What do you think it is about?

b Read the script for Scene 1. Where is the meeting? When is it?

c Work with a partner. Read the scene aloud. What do you think Peter wants to tell Claire? Make a list of possible ideas.

d Work with a partner. Write Scene 2. Describe the scene and write the dialog. Use these questions to help you.

What are Peter and Claire doing?

What does Peter tell Claire?

How does Claire respond?

What do they do next?

e Exchange scenes with another pair and read them. How similar or different are your scenes?

SCRIPT: THE MESSAGE

Scene 1: *There is a table in the middle of a kitchen. Claire is sitting alone at the table. She is eating dinner and looks relaxed. She is wearing jeans and a sweater. The radio is playing in the background. The phone is ringing.*

Peter is off on the side of the stage. He's talking on his cell phone.

Claire: (*reaching for the phone*) Hello.
Peter: Hi, Claire, it's me. (*voice coming from the phone*)
Claire: Oh… (*pausing*), hi. Is this Phil?
Peter: No, it's Peter. Claire, listen, I have something really important to tell you.
Claire: OK. What is it? (*turning down the radio*)
Peter: I don't want to tell you on the phone. We need to meet. (*sounding nervous*)
Claire: OK, it sounds serious. Where do you want to meet?
Peter: Let's meet at the café by your house in ten minutes.
Claire: I'm eating dinner right now. How about in half an hour?
Peter: Claire, this is important. Please come now! (*sounding angry*)
Claire: OK, OK. I'm coming. I'll be there in fifteen minutes.

12 Hot and cold

✔ Weather; seasonal activities; small talk
✔ Adjectives; adverbs of frequency

1 Vocabulary: Months and seasons

a **AUDIO** Listen. Practice saying the months and seasons.

Seasons in the Northern Hemisphere

Winter	Spring	Summer	Fall
December 21	March 21	June 21	September 21
January	April	July	October
February	May	August	November
March 20	June 20	September 20	December 20

Dates in the chart represent the first and last days of the season in each section.

b Which months are part of which seasons where you live?

Example   *June, July, and August are winter months where I live.*

2 Listening

a **AUDIO** Listen. Number the pictures below in the order you hear them.

b Choose the picture that best shows the weather where you live now.

Australia ___

Sweden ___

Japan ___

71

3 ▶ Vocabulary: Weather nouns and adjectives

Read the sentences and complete the chart.

It's cold and snowy in Stockholm today.
It's cloudy and cool in Tokyo.
It's sunny and hot in Sydney.

Noun	Adjective (noun + y)
sun	_____
rain	_rainy_
snow	_____
cloud	_____
fog	_foggy_
wind	_windy_

▼ **Help Desk**

You can use *rain* and *snow* as verbs.

It's raining.

It snows a lot in the winter.

4 ▶ Focus on Grammar

a Look at the chart. Answer the question.

Does the adjective come before or after the noun (for example, *day*)?

Adjectives

It's **sunny** in Sydney.	It's **a sunny** day in Sydney.
It's **warm** in Rome.	Rome is **a warm** city in summer.
It's **cold** today.	Today is **a cold** day.

b Correct the grammar mistakes in these sentences. (More than one answer may be possible.)

1 It's ^a hot day in Mexico City.
   It's a hot day in Mexico City. _____

2 Is cool in London today.
   _____

3 It's a cloudy in Paris this morning.
   _____

4 It's a day snowy in Toronto.
   _____

c Look at the map and the key. Ask and answer questions about the weather in the different cities.

Example   A: *What's the weather like in Anchorage?*
          B: *It's snowy.*

d Talk about the weather in your area today.

Tuesday, November 20

28° Anchorage

sun
rain
snow
clouds
fog
wind

43° Vancouver
55° Seattle
69° San Francisco
72° San Diego

°F °C
hot
warm
cool
cold

Temperatures are in Fahrenheit.

5 KnowHow: Sentence stress

a **AUDIO** Listen to these three sentences.

1 It's a beautiful day.
2 It's cloudy and foggy in London.
3 It's sunny but cold today.

Which kinds of words have the most stress? Circle the correct answer.

a the verb *be*   b words like *and, but*   c nouns and adjectives

b **AUDIO** Practice saying these sentences with the appropriate stress.

1 It's a rainy day.   3 It's sunny and warm today.
2 It's cold and rainy in Seattle.

6 Language in Action: Small talk

a **AUDIO** Put the words into the correct categories. Then listen and complete the conversations.

horrible   nice   wonderful   awful
lovely   beautiful   terrible

POSITIVE	NEGATIVE
	horrible

¹ *Nice*_____ day!
Yes, it's ²_____.

What a ³_____ day!
Yes, it's ⁴_____.

⁵_____ day, isn't it?
Yes, it is.

b Work with a partner. Practice the conversations. Use words for the weather in your area today.

7 ▷ Reading

a Discuss these sentences about the weather on Mars. What do you think?
Write T (true) or F (false).

1 There are no seasons.   —
2 The weather can change very quickly.   —
3 It gets very cold.   —
4 It rains a lot.   —

b Read the article. Were your ideas correct?

TRAVELING TO MARS?
Here's what you need to know!

Surface of Mars.

A vacation on Mars? Does it sound impossible? Some people don't think so. They believe that one day it will be possible. Just in case, here is some weather information to help you prepare for that ultimate trip.

Mars has different seasons like Earth, but they are not equal and are often extreme. Temperatures can change by 40° (22°C) in a few minutes.

Summers last 178 Earth days in the north and 154 Earth days in the south. In the summer, temperatures can reach 60°F (15°C) during the day, but can fall to -90°F (-68°C) the same night. Summers are usually very windy and dusty. There are often dust storms. Dust clouds can be hundreds of miles long and storms sometimes last for days.

Winters are very cold and cloudy. In the south, winter lasts for 183 days. 0°F (-18°C) is a typical high temperature in the daytime. At night, temperatures are sometimes extremely low. Once scientists recorded a temperature of -200°F (-129°C).

On the positive side, you don't usually need an umbrella on Mars. It's often cloudy, but it hardly ever rains. So, you'll need a lot of warm clothes for your trip to Mars, but not a raincoat.

Have a good trip!

Dust clouds on Mars.

c Read the article again and complete the chart.

Seasons on Mars			
	NUMBER OF DAYS	TEMPERATURE	TYPICAL WEATHER
Summer	178 days (north) _____ days (south)		
Winter			

d Some people think that there is life on Mars and that it's possible for humans to travel to Mars. What do you think?

Yes, definitely.   **Possibly.**   **Probably not.**   **No, definitely not.**

Examples *Yes, definitely. I think there is life on Mars…*
           No, definitely not. I don't think there is life on Mars…

8 ▶ Focus on Grammar

a The sentences in the chart show the usual position of some frequency adverbs.

    1   Does the adverb come before or after the verb *be*?

    2   What about other verbs?

Adverbs of frequency	
With be	**With other verbs**
It is **hardly ever** rainy on Mars.	It **hardly ever** rains on Mars.
Temperatures are **sometimes** very low.	Temperatures **sometimes** go very low.

100%
always
usually
often
sometimes
hardly ever
never
0%

b Put the adverb in the correct place in the sentences below.

    1   Summers are very windy. (usually)   _____

    2   There are dust storms. (often)   _____

    3   Storms last for days. (sometimes)   _____

    4   The weather is very extreme. (always)   _____

c Put adverbs in these sentences to make true sentences about where you live. Then compare answers with a partner.

Example   *It's usually hot in Rio de Janeiro in February.*

    1   It's hot in February.   _____

    2   It rains a lot in the summer.   _____

    3   It's cool in the fall.   _____

    4   It snows in the winter.   _____

    5   It's very cold in May.   _____

9 ▶ Speaking

Work in small groups. How do your activities and clothes change at different times of the year? Use these verbs.

wear   go   eat   drink   do   work

Examples   *I often go to the beach on weekends in the summer.*
I usually wear a hat in the winter.
I sometimes work more in September and October.

10 ▶ Writing

a Use your ideas from section 9. Write a paragraph about your life at different times of the year.

Antonio, 25, Barcelona

b Read another student's paragraph. How similar or different are your habits during the year?

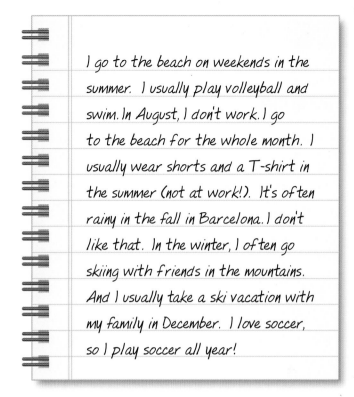

> I go to the beach on weekends in the summer. I usually play volleyball and swim. In August, I don't work. I go to the beach for the whole month. I usually wear shorts and a T-shirt in the summer (not at work!). It's often rainy in the fall in Barcelona. I don't like that. In the winter, I often go skiing with friends in the mountains. And I usually take a ski vacation with my family in December. I love soccer, so I play soccer all year!

11 ▶ Listening: Song

a Can you fill in the missing words to the song? Use the words below.

right see song on me door

b AUDIO Now listen and check.

c AUDIO This song uses colors and the weather to describe being *happy* or *sad*. Listen again. Write *happy* or *sad* in the blanks.

1 I was blue. _____
2 Ev'ry day was a cloudy day for me. _____
3 Skies were gray. _____
4 Blue skies smiling at me. _____
5 Blue days, All of them gone. _____

Now explain the two uses of the word *blue* in the song.

d This classic American song was written in 1926. Why do you think it's still popular today?

Blue Skies
by Irving Berlin

I was blue, just as blue as I could be;
Ev'ry day was a cloudy day for [1] _____
Then good luck came a-knocking at my [2] _____;
Skies were gray, but they're not gray anymore

Blue skies
Smiling at me
Nothing but blue skies
Do I [3] _____.

Bluebirds
Singing a [4] _____,
Nothing but bluebirds
All day long
Never saw the sun shining so bright
Never saw things going so [5] _____.
Noticing the days hurrying by —
When you're in love, my how they fly!

Blue days,
All of them gone —
Nothing but blue skies
From now [6] _____.

Grammar

The Chicago Skyline

Hi Mom,
Here I am, in Chicago. My new job is great, but I'm very busy. I don't have much time to relax. The weather is terrible! It's always windy, and today it's snowing. I like my new apartment. It's in a good neighborhood, and there's a bus stop across the street. I miss you.
Love,
Miriam

Janet Potts
555 Ocean Stre
Miami, Florida

1 Circle the correct answer.

1 Janet Potts lives in _____.
a) Chicago   b) Boston   c) Miami

2 Janet is Miriam's _____.
a) cousin   b) mother   c) daughter

3 Miriam _____ relaxes.
a) usually   b) never   c) hardly ever

4 It is _____ in Chicago.
a) cloudy and rainy
b) windy and snowy
c) rainy and foggy

2 Complete the conversation between Scott and Miriam. Use *there is / isn't, there are, Is there…?*, or *Are there..?*

S: So, tell me about your new apartment. How many bedrooms are there?

M: Well, there are two bedrooms.

S: ¹_____*Is there*_____ a dining room?

M: No, ²_____, but ³_____ a large living room.

S: It sounds nice. ⁴_____ a lot of stores nearby?

M: Yes, ⁵_____, and ⁶_____ two or three cafés on my street.

S: ⁷_____ a subway stop in the neighborhood?

M: No, ⁸_____. I take the bus to work.

3 Circle the correct answer. Simple present or present continuous?

K: Hello, Miriam. This is Karen, Scott's wife.

M: Oh. Hello, Karen.

K: ¹(Are you eating / Do you eat) dinner?

M: No, I'm not. I ²(relax / 'm relaxing) in front of the TV.

K: Oh, good. I ³(call / 'm calling) about dinner on Friday. Are you free?

M: Yes, I am. I hardly ever ⁴(go / am going) out on Friday nights.

K: Great. We usually ⁵(eat / are eating) about 7:00. So come around 6:00 or 6:30.

4 Look at the chart. Write sentences, questions, and answers with *can*.
✓ = yes; ✗ = no.

Examples
Miriam can program a computer.
Scott can't dance.
Can Karen and Scott play golf?

	Miriam	**Karen**	**Scott**
dance	✓	✓	✗
play the guitar	✗	✗	✓
play golf	✗	✓	✓
program a computer	✓	✗	✓
cook	✗	✓	✗

5 Write sentences with *always, usually, often, sometimes, hardly ever,* or *never*. Use each word once.
(0% = never; 100% = always)

Miami
1 cold / 10%
   It is hardly ever cold in Miami.
2 rains / 60% / in September
   _____
3 sunny / 100% / in the spring
   _____

Chicago
4 snows / 0% / in July
   _____
5 foggy / 40% / in the morning
   _____
6 windy / 80% / in the fall
   _____

Vocabulary

6 Put the letters in order to make words. Then add more words to each set.

places	months	sports	rooms
nakb (bank)	enJu	cie tasking	tharmoob
tennssawd	gutusA	cocers	tenchik
dgruserto	Fuyarebr	ebalsalb	egaarg
_____	_____	_____	_____

Recycling Center 🔄

7 Complete with *-s, -'s,* or *N*. (*N* = nothing). Note: The *-'s* can be a contraction of *is* or a possessive.

Scott and Karen Martin live __x__¹ in Chicago. Scott __'s__² Miriam ____³ boss. He ____⁴ a computer programmer, and he work ____⁵ with the new people in the office. He love ____⁶ his job. Scott and Karen often invite ____⁷ friends home for dinner. Karen love ____⁸ to cook, and she like ____⁹ to meet new people. Miriam ____¹⁰ eating dinner with them tonight.

8 Look at the *'s* endings in the paragraph above.

1 Which endings are contractions?
2 Which is possessive?

Fun Spot

Can you solve this puzzle?

What is always coming but never arrives?

Hint: moworrot

13 Take care of yourself

✔ Computer language; parts of the body; ailments and remedies
✔ *Should / shouldn't*; modifiers

1 ▸ Vocabulary: Parts of the body

AUDIO Listen. Practice saying the parts of the body.

head
eye
ear
neck
shoulder
back
arm
hand
knee
leg
foot

Do

- **Use a good chair.**
- _____ 1
- _____ 2
- _____ 3

Don't

- **Don't sit too close to the screen.**
- _____ 4
- **Don't sit too long. Take breaks.**

> ▼ **Help Desk**
>
> You usually use possessive adjectives (for example, *my* or *your*) with parts of the body.
>
> *Relax **your** hands.*
>
> Is this different in your language?

2 ▸ Listening

a Look at the poster above. Find a part of the picture that relates to each of these phrases.

1. cross your legs
2. keep your feet flat on the floor
3. keep your hands and arms relaxed
4. sit an arm's length away

b **AUDIO** Listen. Then complete the poster with the phrases from 2a.

3 ▶ Focus on Grammar

a Look at the chart. Then make sentences with *should* or *shouldn't*. Use the poster on page 79.

Example   *Your chair should support your back. You shouldn't cross your legs.*

Should / shouldn't (advice / suggestions)	
Affirmative statements	**Negative statements**
I You He / She **should** sit up straight. We They	I You He / She **shouldn't** sit in that chair. We They
Questions	**Answers**
Should I take a break now? What **should** I do?	**Yes**, you **should**. **No**, you **shouldn't**. You **should** sit up straight.

b Complete the sentences. Use an expression below and *should* or *shouldn't*.

sit up straight   take a break   sit too close to the screen   cross her legs   use a good chair

1 They look tired.   They *should take a break*____.
2 She has a bad knee!   She _____.
3 Oh, my back!   You _____.
4 This chair isn't very comfortable.   You _____.
5 My eyes are tired.   You _____.

4 ▶ Vocabulary: Ailments and remedies

a **AUDIO** Listen. Practice saying the ailments (row 1) and remedies (row 2).

I'm tired.   I have a cold.   I have a headache.   I have a stomachache.   I'm stressed out.   My back hurts.

take some aspirin   drink hot liquids and stay warm   try to relax more   go to bed early   exercise   see a doctor

b Which remedies are good for each ailment? Compare answers with a partner. (Different answers are possible.)

Example   A: *I have a cold.*
          B: *You should see a doctor.*

5 ▶ *KnowHow*: Organizing vocabulary

a Organizing words according to a topic is a good way to remember them. Look at the example diagram. Then make two more diagrams. Choose from the following or use your own ideas.

colors   weather   clothes   food   ailments   remedies   action verbs

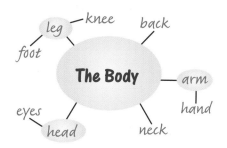

b Compare your diagrams with other students.

6 ▶ Language in Action: Giving advice

a **AUDIO** Listen. Check the expressions you hear in the conversation.

GIVING ADVICE	RESPONDING
__ You should…	__ You're probably right.
__ You shouldn't…	__ That's a good idea.
__ Why don't you…?	

Laura: What's the matter?
Ray: My back hurts!
Laura: You shouldn't sit so long.
       Why don't you stretch or exercise?
Ray: That's a good idea.
Laura: I hope you feel better.
Ray: Thanks.

b Work with a partner. Practice the conversation. Use different ailments and remedies from 4a.

Example A: *What's the matter?*
         B: *My _____ hurts!…*

▼ **Help Desk**

If someone doesn't feel well, you can say:

I hope you feel better.

7 ▶ Reading

a Discuss these questions.

1 Do you think it's possible to use computers too much?
2 What problems come from using computers a lot?

b Read the article. Are your ideas similar to or different from those in the article?

Computers: How much is too much?

Work, computer games, the Internet—everyone uses computers these days. For most people, this isn't a problem. They work or play games, and then they turn off the computer.

But, some people can't stop playing computer games or using the Internet. This problem can affect jobs, relationships, and studies. It's possible that about 6 percent of computer users have this problem.

Pete is a 20-year-old university student. He loves computer games. He says he sometimes plays games for ten hours a day on weekends.

He says that it can be difficult to turn off the computer and do other things.

"I play computer games all day, and then I'm too tired to do anything else. My friends don't like it. I forget to call them, and they say they never see me. So, now I'm trying to study and see my friends first and then turn on the computer."

Why are computers so addictive? Researchers say the visual impact—color, graphics, movement—is very powerful. The endless information and fast response also make them very attractive.

And, if you have a problem? Researchers say you shouldn't use the computer every day. You should develop other interests and talk to friends and family.

c Read the article again. Write T (true) or F (false).

1 Most computer users are addicted to computer games. —
2 Pete sometimes can't stop playing computer games. —
3 Pete's friends are not happy about the time he spends on the computer. —
4 Most people don't like the color, graphics, and movement on computers. —
5 If you think you have a problem, you should develop other interests. —

d Fill in the blanks with expressions from the list.

turn on   researcher   be careful   addictive   turn off

1 I think chocolate is _____! I eat too much of it!
2 Please, _____. Don't talk on the phone when you are driving.
3 When I leave the office, I _____ my computer and close the door.
4 Dr. Ann Thompson is a _____. She studies remedies for headaches.
5 I usually get home about 7:00. Then I _____ the TV and watch my favorite programs.

8 ► In Conversation

AUDIO What's the problem with the table?
Listen. Then read.

Pete: Hey! Jerry! Don't put that computer on that table!
Jerry: Huh? Why not? What's the problem?
Pete: The table's too small.
Jerry: Yes, you're right. This monitor is pretty big. How about this desk? Can I put it here?
Pete: Sure. That's fine. Thanks.

9 ► Focus on Grammar

a Look at the chart. Answer the questions.

1 Which word means "more than is good in the situation"? (*too* or *very*)
2 Can you put these sentences in order? (Least = 1)
The table is kind of small. ___
The table is very small. ___
The table isn't very small. ___

Modifiers		
I'm You're He's / She's / It's We're They're	**too** **very / really** **pretty / kind of** **not very**	tired. big. relaxed. small.

▼ **Help Desk**

The modifiers *pretty* and *kind of* are more informal than the others.

b Circle the correct words.

1 You should wear a light jacket. It's (really / kind of) cold today.
2 It's (too / not very) hot to play tennis. Let's go swimming.
3 Nina is (really / not very) relaxed. She's always stressed out.
4 I am (very / too) tired, but let's go to the party anyway. I can sleep tomorrow.

c Complete the chart for you. Write sentences. Then compare answers with a partner.

Example   *I usually go to bed very late. I'm not very tired today.*

	too	very / really	pretty / kind of	not very
1 How late do you usually go to bed?		(✓)		
2 How early do you get up?				
3 How tired are you today?				
4 How stressed out are you today?				
5 How relaxed are you in general?				

10 ▶ Reading, Writing, and Speaking: An advice column

a Read the letters. Which problem do you think is most serious?

ASK JENNA

A Dear Jenna,
My boyfriend works hard and has a really good job in advertising. The problem is that he works too hard. He always has his laptop computer with him. He turns on his computer and says he has to do "a little work." Then he doesn't talk to me for hours! I love him, but I'm getting pretty tired of his work. What should I do?
—Virginia—

B Dear Jenna,
I'm kind of worried about my 14-year-old daughter. She uses the Internet and plays computer games every day. I know she uses the Internet for homework, but I'm worried about what else she's doing on the computer. She has the computer in her bedroom and she closes the door, so I can't see what she's doing. Am I worrying too much?
—Pat—

C Dear Jenna,
A few months ago, I met a nice woman in a chat room online. I live in Australia, and she lives in Hong Kong. We started talking, and now we talk almost every day. I really like her. The problem is that she's coming to Australia next month on business, and she wants to meet. I'm really nervous about this. What if she doesn't like me in person or if she's completely different in person? Should I do this?
—Simon—

b Work in small groups. Discuss possible advice for the letters.

c Read the advice. Which letter does it go with? Do you agree with the advice?

Dear_____,
No, you're not! You shouldn't ignore this. The Internet is a very useful thing for studying, but there is also a lot that is not for a teenager. I think you should move the computer out to the family room or kitchen so you can see what she's doing. Why don't you do some things on the computer with her? Help her with her homework or play a game with her. If you don't know anything about computers, you should learn. Ask her to teach you!

d Choose one of the other problems. Write a letter of advice.

Include:
  –one or two suggestions
  –a reason for your answer

e Read other students' advice. Who has the best advice for each problem?

14 *It was fantastic!*

✔ Describing events in the past; responding to a story
✔ Simple past of *be* and of regular and irregular verbs

 In Conversation

AUDIO Listen. Then read. Match the conversations (1–3) to the photographs (A–C).

1

A: How was work today?
B: It was terrible. We were very busy, and my boss wasn't happy. Ugh.

2

A: How was your whitewater rafting trip?
B: It was fantastic! The weather was pretty bad, but the rafting was really exciting!

3

A: How was the party last night?
B: It was fun! There were a lot of nice people. The music was good, and the food was delicious.

2 Vocabulary: Adjectives and nouns

a Look at the conversations again. Which words are used to describe these nouns?

1 weather   _bad_   4 food   _____
2 person / people   _____   5 trip   _____
3 music   _____

b Cross out the word which isn't usually used with each noun.

1 nice	terrible	~~important~~	**weather**
2 busy	long	famous	**person**
3 delicious	good	busy	**food**
4 small	beautiful	terrible	**day**
5 loud	good	big	**music**
6 exciting	delicious	fantastic	**trip**

c Use adjectives to describe these things.

the weather today   last Saturday   your best friend   your last trip

85

3 ▷ Focus on Grammar

Look at the chart. Then complete the conversation below.

Simple past: *be*	
Statements	**Questions and answers**

I **was** (**wasn't**)
You **were** (**weren't**)
He / She / It **was** (**wasn't**)   busy.
We **were** (**weren't**)
They **were** (**weren't**)
	Were you busy?
	    Yes, I was. No, I wasn't.
	Was she busy?
	    Yes, she was. No, she wasn't.
	How **were** your classes?
	    They **were** very interesting.

Note: wasn't = was not weren't = were not	

A: How <u>¹ *was*</u> work?

B: It ²_____ terrible! First, I ³_____ late and my boss ⁴_____ (not) happy. Then, the usual cook ⁵_____ (not) there. She ⁶_____ sick, so there ⁷_____ a different cook. He ⁸_____ (not) very good and people ⁹_____ (not) happy with the food. There ¹⁰_____ a lot of people and it ¹¹_____ very busy all day. There ¹²_____ (not) even time for a break.

4 ▷ Language in Action: Responding to information

a **AUDIO** Listen. Complete the conversations with the expressions below.

Oh really?   That's good.   That's too bad.

A: How was your weekend?
B: It was terrible.
A: ¹_____
B: I was sick all weekend.
A: ²_____

C: How was your vacation?
D: It was wonderful.
C: ³_____
D: Yes, the weather was great and the beaches were beautiful.
C: ⁴_____

b Practice the conversations with a partner. Use the ideas below or your own ideas.

your day   work   school   classes   yesterday   last weekend   last week

In Conversation

AUDIO What did Liza find in the apartment? Listen. Then read.

Tom: You look tired.
Liza: I am. I just moved into a new apartment.
Tom: Oh really?
Liza: Yes, yesterday I cleaned, painted, and decorated all day.
Tom: It sounds like a lot of work.
Liza: Yes, it was, but some friends came over and helped me.
Tom: That's good.
Liza: We found something a little strange, though.
Tom: Really? What?
Liza: We found some really old letters in the back of a closet. I read one. They're love letters to someone named Clara.
Tom: How interesting!
Liza: I know. I'd like to return the letters, though. They're important to someone.

6 **Focus on Grammar**

a Look at the chart. How do you form the simple past of regular verbs?

Simple past: Affirmative statements						
Regular verbs			*Irregular verbs*			
I	moved in	yesterday.	I	**came** over	last weekend.	
She	clean**ed** the apartment	last night.	We	**found** some letters	on Saturday.	
They	paint**ed**	all day.	You	**read** the letters	this morning.	

b AUDIO List the present and past forms of the verbs. Listen and check your answers.

wrote	threw	took	knew	went	met	said	read
found	want	had	say	find	know	write	put
go	meet	put	read	have	wanted	take	throw

c Fill in the blanks with the past of *come, want, be, move, meet, help, work,* and *have.*

Hi!

I ¹ _wanted_ to send you my new address. I ² _____ in last weekend. My brother and some friends ³ _____ me move. It ⁴ _____ a lot of work! We ⁵ _____ all day and then I ⁶ _____ a little party in the evening. My neighbors ⁷ _____ so I ⁸ _____ them. They're really nice.

7 KnowHow: Pronunciation of -ed endings

a **AUDIO** Listen. Which simple past verb has an extra syllable?

1 I worked. I worked on Saturday.
2 I cleaned. I cleaned on Saturday.
3 I painted. I painted on Saturday.

b **AUDIO** Look at this explanation: The *-ed* ending is pronounced / ɪd / after / t / or / d /.

Now listen. Then practice reading the text aloud to a partner.

On Friday, I worked in the apartment. I cleaned all day. Then I watched TV — I needed a break!

On Saturday, I painted and decorated all day. I finished at 9 p.m.

On Sunday, I moved in! Joe visited. He cooked dinner.

8 Listening

a **AUDIO** Listen. Did Liza find the person the letters belonged to?

b **AUDIO** Listen again. Write T (true) or F (false).

1 The old man knew Clara and Albert.
—

2 The old man knew where they moved.
—

3 Liza used the phone book to find the family.
—

4 Liza talked to Albert.
—

5 Liza returned the letters.
—

6 Albert was in Europe when he wrote the letters.
—

c Did you (or someone you know) ever find something unusual? What was it? What happened?

9 Reading

a Read the story. Which of these sentences is false?

1 Harold Myers doesn't like to go on cruises.
2 Harold received letters from people far away.
3 The bottles floated long distances.

A Message in a Bottle

Harold and his wife, Lois, took a Caribbean cruise in 1987. Harold took three bottles with him. He wrote messages in English and Spanish, and put each message in a bottle with a dollar. The dollar, his note explained, was to pay for postage for a response. Harold threw the three bottles into the water.

Soon after he returned home from the cruise, he received a letter. A French tourist found the bottle on the beach on St. Bart's, an island 30 miles away from where Harold threw it in the water. Harold was excited. "I really didn't expect to hear from anybody at all," he said. Another bottle floated for almost 2,000 miles and survived a hurricane. A tourist recovered it near Belize.

The bottles were now Harold's hobby. He threw more bottles into the sea on an Alaskan cruise, and again a few years later near

Many people throw messages into the ocean, but Harold Myers is one of the lucky few to receive responses!

Acapulco. Both times, people found his bottles and wrote him letters. Then, in 1996, while on a cruise off the coast of Mexico, Harold threw in three more bottles. Twenty-two months later a fisherman wrote to say he recovered the bottle in the sea near the Philippines. The bottle traveled at least 7,000 miles from the other side of the Pacific!

b Read the story again. Put the events in order.

___ A tourist in Belize found a bottle with a message in it.
___ Harold threw bottles into the water near Alaska.
___ A French tourist wrote him a letter.
___ A fisherman found a bottle after 22 months.
___ Harold threw three bottles into the ocean in 1987.

c Find a word for each definition. (1) = paragraph number.

1 answer (1) _____
2 amount of money used to mail something (1) _____
3 to find something that someone lost or threw away (2/3) _____
4 something you do for fun in your free time (3) _____

d What do you think of this article? Do you know any other stories like this?

10 ▶ Speaking and Writing

a Read the message in the bottle. How does Nick start the message? How does he end it?

> 12 Dune Street
> Seaside Heights, NJ
>
> Dear Finder,
> I threw this bottle into the Atlantic Ocean from a beach in New Jersey, in the
> United States. Please write to me if you find this message. Please tell me when
> you found it and where you found it. I want to know how far it traveled. Also,
> please tell me something about you and your life!
>
> Sincerely,
>
> Nick Treglio

b Write a response to the message above. Say when you found the bottle and where you found it. Give some information about your life. Use real information or use the pictures and your imagination.

c Work in small groups. Read your responses aloud. Answer these questions. How are they the same? How are they different? Which ones are unusual?

15 Extraordinary lives

✔ Life events; expressing certainty
✔ Simple past: Negative statements and questions

1 Vocabulary: Life events

a Write the events under the correct picture.

get married   start school   get a job

(be) born

1 _____

2 _____

3 _____

have children

b **AUDIO** What are the simple past forms of these verbs? Listen and check.

2 Listening

a **AUDIO** Listen. How was Justine Kerfoot's life different from her plans?

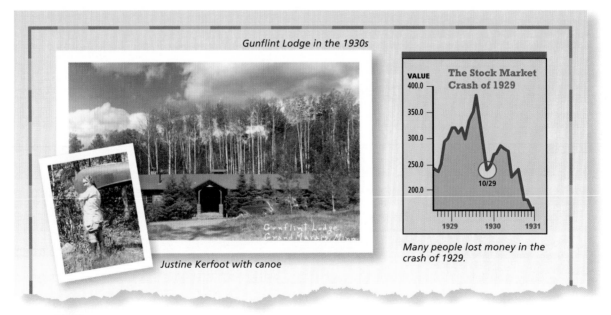
Gunflint Lodge in the 1930s

Justine Kerfoot with canoe

The Stock Market Crash of 1929

Many people lost money in the crash of 1929.

b **AUDIO** Listen again. Circle the correct answer.

1 Justine was born in (Illinois / New York).
2 Justine's family had (one / more than one) house.
3 Justine graduated with a degree in (education / zoology).
4 Justine planned to be a (teacher / doctor).

3 ▶ Focus on Grammar

a Look at the grammar chart and circle the correct word in the sentence below.

Use the (past / base) form of the main verb after *didn't*.

Simple past: Negative statements		
I You He / She We They	**didn't** (did not)	**have** a lot of money. **stay** in Illinois. **become** a doctor.

b Make negative sentences to correct the statements.

1 Justine's family had three houses before the stock market crash.
   Justine's family didn't have three houses before the stock market crash.

2 The stock market crashed in 1930.
   _____

3 Her family had a lot of money after the stock market crash.
   _____

4 Justine stayed in Chicago.
   _____

5 She became a doctor.
   _____

c Work with a partner. Which of these things <u>didn't</u> you do yesterday? Tell your partner.

watch TV	talk on the phone	visit an old friend	get up early
get up late	go to the movies	read a book	play a game
eat dinner	have a big breakfast	have a light lunch	

Example   *I didn't have a big breakfast.*

4 ▶ Vocabulary: Years

a **AUDIO** Listen and practice.

1900   1907   1993   2001   2050

b **AUDIO** Say these years. Then listen and check.

1904   1910   1980   1995   2000   2005   2031

> ▼ **Help Desk**
>
> Use *in* with the year and the month, but *on* with the exact date and the month.
>
> *Alex was born in 1981.*
>
> *Alex was born in January.*
>
> *Alex was born on January 3, 1981.*

5 ▶ Reading

a Look at the pictures and the title. Then read the article. Why was Justine a "true pioneer"?

A True Pioneer

Justine was a 21-year-old city girl when she moved to her family's small fishing camp, called Gunflint Lodge, in the wilderness of Northern Minnesota. She and her family lived there after they lost their money and their other homes in the Depression.

The lodge didn't have running water or electricity when they arrived. Justine learned how to hunt and fish from the Native Americans who lived in the area. In the winter, she traveled by dogsled for days or even a week at a time.

She got married in 1934. She and her husband, Bill Kerfoot, had three children. They worked very hard to make the lodge a successful business. After a fire in 1953, Justine and Bill rebuilt the lodge in only a few months. Justine made most of the new furniture herself. It was sometimes difficult, but Justine and Bill made the lodge a success.

In her later years, Justine drove across Africa and traveled to the Amazon and Antarctica. She continued to hunt, fish, canoe, and ride dogsleds when she was over 80 years old. She wrote three books about her life.

Her life definitely didn't turn out as planned, but it was an amazing life.

b Read again. Write T (true) or F (false).

1 Justine and her family went to Gunflint Lodge for a vacation. ___
2 There were no electric lights at Gunflint Lodge when they arrived. ___
3 Justine didn't know how to hunt or fish when she arrived. ___
4 Justine and Bill had two sons and two daughters. ___
5 It took a long time to rebuild the lodge after the fire. ___
6 Justine didn't do adventurous things when she was old. ___

c What do you think? What was unusual about Justine's life? Talk about someone you know who has (or had) an unusual life.

6 ▶ *KnowHow*: Reading tips

a Look at these suggestions.

1 Look at the pictures. Think about the topic before you read.
2 First, read the whole text quickly.
3 Don't focus on every word. Use key words to help you understand the main ideas.
4 Read the text more than once.

b Look back at section 5. How did you apply suggestions 1–4 as you read?

7 ▶ In Conversation

AUDIO Who is Susie asking about? Listen. Then read.

Susie: Famous people.
First question: Where was Albert Einstein born, Germany or Switzerland?

Phil: Hmm, let me think. It's probably Germany. Yes, Germany.

Susie: Yes, that's right. He was born there in 1879. Next: Did he win a Nobel Prize for his work?

Phil: Oh, that's easy. Yes, he did.

Susie: Yes. Next question: Did he have children?

Phil: Umm… I'm not sure. I know he was married…. I'll say "Yes."

Susie: Yes, he had children. Now, a bonus question for five extra points.

Phil: OK.

Susie: How many sons did he have?

Phil: I don't know. Hmm. I'm guessing…four?

Susie: No, sorry. He had two sons.

8 ▶ Focus on Grammar

a Look at the chart. Find examples of questions and answers in the conversation in section 7.

Simple past: Questions		
Questions	*Answers*	
Did he **win** a Nobel Prize?	Yes, he **did.**	No, he **didn't.**
When **did** he **win** it?	In 1921.	
Did he **have** children?	Yes, he **did.**	No, he **didn't.**
How many children **did** he **have**?	Two.	

b Prepare questions for an interview about a real person from another generation. (Think about people you know of in your family or community.)

Examples *When was(name) born? Did (he / she) go to high school?*

1 When / born?
2 Where / born?
3 go / university (or high school)?
4 When / graduate?
5 get married? (If *yes*, ask *When…*?)
6 have children? (If *yes*, ask *How many…*?)
7 get a job? (When? / Where?)

c Work with a partner. Use your questions from 8b. **A**, ask about your partner's person. **B**, answer **A**'s questions. Then change roles.

9 ▶ Language in Action: Degrees of certainty

a **AUDIO** Listen to the conversation in section 7 again. Focus on Phil. Which expressions does he use?

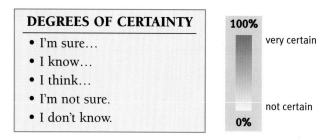

DEGREES OF CERTAINTY

- I'm sure…
- I know…
- I think…
- I'm not sure.
- I don't know.

100% very certain

not certain 0%

b Work with a partner. Write four questions about famous people or current events. **A**, ask a question. **B**, answer the question. Use an expression from the list.

Example   A: *Where was Pablo Picasso born?*
            B: *Hmm. I'm not sure. I think he was born in Spain. Or was it France?*

10 ▶ Writing

a Read the paragraph about a famous person. Who was this person?

WHO WAS SHE?

She was born in Albania on August 27, 1910. The whole world knew her for her work with the poor. She entered the order of the Sisters of Our Lady of Loreto at the age of 18 and taught in Calcutta. In 1946, she started her work with dying people and opened an orphanage. In 1950, she started a charity to help very poor people. She received the Nobel Peace Prize in 1979. She died in 1997.

b Think of a famous person. Write a paragraph about the person's life, but don't write the name. Look at the pictures on this page for ideas or use your own ideas.

c Read your paragraph to other students. Can they guess who the person is?

11 ▶ Speaking

Work in small groups. Write six important years in your life. Ask and answer questions with the people in the group.

Example   A's list: 1983, 1994, …

B: *Were you born in 1983?*
A: *No, I wasn't.*
C: *Did you start school in 1983?*
A: *Yes, I did.*
D: *Where did you go to school?*

16 Let's celebrate!

✔ Festivals and celebrations; invitations
✔ Future with *be going to* + verb; subject-object pronouns

1 ▸ Vocabulary: Celebrations

a Match the words (1–4) and definitions (a–d).

wedding anniversary

wedding

graduation

birthday

1	birthday	__	a the ceremony when you get married
2	wedding anniversary	__	b the day that you were born
3	graduation	__	c the same day that you got married
4	wedding	__	d the ceremony when you finish school or university

b Make a list of things you do for each celebration. Use the ideas below. Then compare lists with other students.

Example *birthday: have a party, give and get presents*

have a party	give and get presents
take pictures	wear special clothes
have a special meal	have a special ceremony
get together with family or friends	go out to a restaurant
send a card	dance

2 ▶ Reading

a Read the article. What are these people going to celebrate?

Voices in the street...

Everyone has different things to celebrate every day.
We asked two people, *"What are you going to celebrate soon?"*

**Adam Rafitz, 22
San Diego, California**

My new job! I finally got a job in journalism, and I'm really happy. I start next week, so I'm going to celebrate this weekend. My girlfriend's going to take me out for dinner at my favorite restaurant.

**Keesha Peters, 39
Boston, Massachusetts**

My husband and I are going to celebrate our 16th wedding anniversary next week. We're going to take a trip to celebrate, but I don't know where we're going. My husband wants to surprise me!

b What other events do you celebrate?

3 ▶ Focus on Grammar

a Look at the chart and circle the correct ending for this sentence.

Use *be going to* for (future plans / something happening now.)

Now find three more examples of *be going to* in section 2.

Future: *be going to* + verb		
Statements		*Questions and answers*

I'm (I'm not)
You're (You aren't)
He / She / It's
  (He / She / It isn't)
We're (We aren't)
They're (They aren't)
	going to be on time.	**Are** you **going to** celebrate?
		  Yes, I **am.** No, I'm not.
		Is he **going to** celebrate?
		  Yes, he **is.** No, he **isn't.**
		What **are** they **going to** celebrate?
		  Their wedding anniversary.

b Fill in the missing word in each sentence.

  to   are   is   going

1 We ^*are* going to celebrate this weekend.
2 Graciela going to get presents.
3 When is Frank to start his new job?
4 My friends are going have a party.

c Talk about things you're going to do and things you're not going to do...

  this evening   tomorrow   next weekend

Example *I'm not going to watch TV this evening. I'm going to...*

4 ▶ In Conversation

AUDIO Who is going to buy a CD for Sam? Listen. Then read.

Amy: Hey, Ben! Sam's birthday is next week. What are you going to give him?
Ben: I don't know. Do you have any ideas?
Amy: Well, he likes music. What about a CD?
Ben: That's a good idea.
Amy: The new *Kayaks* CD would be good.
Ben: Great. Now I know what to buy.
Amy: Hey, wait! What am *I* going to give him?

5 ▶ Focus on Grammar

a Look at the examples and complete the chart.

*What are you going to give **Sam**?* ➔ *What are you going to give **him**?*
*He likes the **Kayaks**.* ➔ *He likes **them**.*
*I'm going to buy the **CD**.* ➔ *I'm going to buy **it**.*

Subject-object pronouns					
I	**me**	She	**her**	We	**us**
You	**you**	He	_____	You	**you**
		It	_____	They	_____

b Fill in the blanks with object pronouns.

1 Jon is making a birthday cake for Lori.
   Can you help ___*him*___?
   —Yes. Is he making _____ now?
2 Rosa called. Please call _____.
3 I need a present. Can you help _____?

4 Do you know Liz and Mike?
   —No, I don't know _____.
5 We're planning a party. Do you want to help _____?
   —Sure, I'll help _____.

6 ▶ Listening

a **AUDIO** Listen to Amy and Jamie talk about Sam's birthday. Number the items in the order you hear them.

a tennis racket and some balls   —   a CD   —
a gift certificate   —   a book —

b **AUDIO** Listen again. What do they decide to buy? Who is the present going to be from?

c What kinds of things do you like to receive as presents?

Vocabulary: Ordinal numbers

Look at the chart. Which ordinal numbers *don't* end in *-th*?

Ordinal Numbers

first	1st	sixth	6th	eleventh	11th	sixteenth	16th	twenty-first	21st
second	2nd	seventh	7th	twelfth	12th	seventeenth	17th	twenty-second	22nd
third	3rd	eighth	8th	thirteenth	13th	eighteenth	18th	...	
fourth	4th	ninth	9th	fourteenth	14th	nineteenth	19th	thirtieth	30th
fifth	5th	tenth	10th	fifteenth	15th	twentieth	20th	thirty-first	31st

8 *KnowHow*: **Pronunciation**

a AUDIO Listen. Practice saying the ordinal numbers.

b Say the date: today / tomorrow / yesterday.

> ▼ **Help Desk**
>
> Write days like this:
>
> *June 15, 2005* Or *6 / 15 / 05*
>
> You say dates like this:
>
> *June fifteenth* (or *the fifteenth of June*), *two thousand five.*

9 **Language in Action: Invitations**

a AUDIO Listen. Which day are Sergio and Lisa going to go to the music festival?

Sergio: Would you like to go to the music festival?
Lisa: I'd love to. When is it?
Sergio: It's on Friday, June 15th.
Lisa: I'm sorry, I have plans on the 15th.
Sergio: Well, it's also on Saturday, the 16th.
    Do you want to go then?
Lisa: Yes, that'd be great.

INVITING	ACCEPTING	REFUSING
Would you like to…?	OK.	I'm sorry. I can't.
Do you want to…?	I'd love to.	I'd like to, but I have plans.
	Yes, that'd be great.	

b Work with a partner. Invite your partner to one of these events. Use expressions from the chart above.

International Art
Calhoun Beach
June 1st–4th

Festival Spring Party
Lake Street
May 30th–31st

10 ▶ Reading

a Read the article. Match the pictures to the festivals.

Festivals Around the World

Las Fallas

Las Fallas is a festival in Valencia, Spain, to celebrate spring and the feast of San José. Artists make giant figures of paper, wood, and paint and then burn them in the festival. The figures are huge (some are almost five stories tall!), and they usually represent a famous personality or fantasy figure. On March 19th, the streets of Valencia are filled with fire and noise.

Vasant Panchami

In January or February, Hindus in many parts of India celebrate the coming of spring with the festival of Vasant Panchami, the birthday of the goddess of learning, wisdom, and fine arts. Young children are encouraged to write the letters of the alphabet for the first time. People wear yellow clothes, make special rice, and fly kites.

Sapporo Yuki Matsuri

In February, in Sapporo, Japan, artists and ice sculptors make very large ice sculptures. These include models of animals, such as whales. There are also models of famous buildings like the Egyptian pyramids and the Great Wall of China. Visitors can even walk around in some of these sculptures. Tourists come from around the world to see the ice kingdom and take part in special games and activities.

b Read the article again. Complete the chart.

	Las Fallas Valencia, Spain	Vasant Panchami India	Snow Festival Sapporo, Japan
When?	March		
Why?	to celebrate spring and the feast of San José		
What do they do?			

c Find these words in the text above. Then choose the correct definition.
(1) = paragraph number.

1 *burn* (1) a to destroy something with fire b to make something
2 *huge* (1) a very small b very big
3 *noise* (1) a something you see b something you hear
4 *take part in* (3) a to participate in b to watch

d Which festival would you like to go to? Do you know of any other interesting or unusual festivals? Discuss.

11 Speaking and Writing

a Work in small groups. Think of three different festivals in your country. Discuss them and complete the chart.

	1. _____	2. _____	3. _____
When?			
Why?			
What do you do?			

b Choose one celebration. Use your notes and write a paragraph about it.

c Read another student's description of the same celebration. How similar or different are your descriptions?

12 Listening: Song

a Try to put these lyrics in the correct place in the song.

> And forever we'll be free
> 'Til the music fades away
> It's gonna be a perfect day
> Peace and love is what we dream of

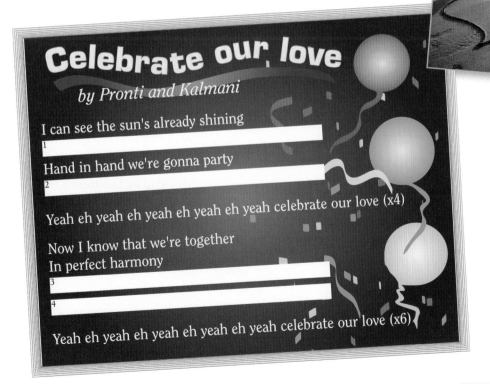

Celebrate our love
by Pronti and Kalmani

I can see the sun's already shining
1 _____

Hand in hand we're gonna party
2 _____

Yeah eh yeah eh yeah eh yeah eh yeah celebrate our love (x4)

Now I know that we're together
In perfect harmony
3 _____
4 _____

Yeah eh yeah eh yeah eh yeah eh yeah celebrate our love (x6)

b **AUDIO** Now listen to the song and check.

c What is the singer celebrating? What other songs do you associate with celebrations?

> ▼ *Help Desk*
>
> People often use *gonna* for *going to* in informal situations, especially songs.

Grammar

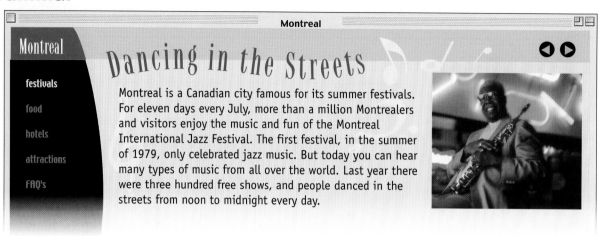

Montreal

Dancing in the Streets

Montreal is a Canadian city famous for its summer festivals. For eleven days every July, more than a million Montrealers and visitors enjoy the music and fun of the Montreal International Jazz Festival. The first festival, in the summer of 1979, only celebrated jazz music. But today you can hear many types of music from all over the world. Last year there were three hundred free shows, and people danced in the streets from noon to midnight every day.

festivals
food
hotels
attractions
FAQ's

1 ▸ Write the answers.

1 Where is Montreal?
   _____

2 How many people go to the festival?
   _____

3 When was the first festival?
   _____

4 How many free shows were there last year?
   _____

2 ▸ Complete the conversation. Fill in the blanks with *be going to* + verb.

Joe: ¹ *Are you going to go* _____ (you / go) to Newport this year?

Pat: No, I'm not. I ² _____ (go) to the Montreal Jazz Festival with my sister Katy.

Joe: That's a pretty big festival. You should reserve a hotel room soon.

Pat: Oh, we don't need a hotel room. We ³_____ (stay) with my sister's friend, Pierre.

Joe: When ⁴_____ (you / buy) the tickets?

Pat: We don't need tickets. We ⁵_____ (see) the free shows.

3 ▸ Complete the conversation with *is*, *should*, *do*, *when*, or *can*.

Pierre: Hello?

Katy: Hi Pierre, it's Katy. How are you?

Pierre: I'm great. So, ¹ *when* are you going to come to Montreal?

Katy: We're going to take the bus on Friday morning. ²_____ we stay at your place?

Pierre: Sure. ³_____ Pat going to come, too?

Katy: Yes, she is. ⁴_____ we bring some food?

Pierre: No, that's OK. ⁵_____ you want me to meet you at the bus?

Katy: That would be really nice. See you on Friday. Bye.

4 ▸ Complete these FAQs (Frequently Asked Questions) about the Montreal Jazz Festival. Use *should*.

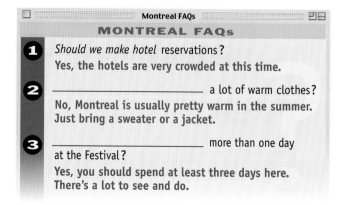

Montreal FAQs

MONTREAL FAQs

❶ *Should we make hotel reservations?*
Yes, the hotels are very crowded at this time.

❷ _____ a lot of warm clothes?
No, Montreal is usually pretty warm in the summer. Just bring a sweater or a jacket.

❸ _____ more than one day at the Festival?
Yes, you should spend at least three days here. There's a lot to see and do.

5 Read Pat's notes for her journal. Then write the entries in her journal. Use the past tense.

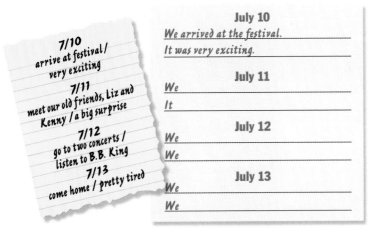

7/10
arrive at festival /
very exciting

7/11
meet our old friends, Liz and
Kenny / a big surprise

7/12
go to two concerts /
listen to B.B. King

7/13
come home / pretty tired

July 10
We arrived at the festival.
It was very exciting.

July 11
We _____
It _____

July 12
We _____
We _____

July 13
We _____
We _____

6 Complete the letter with the correct object pronoun: *you, him, her, us, them,* or *it.*

Dear Joe,
Liz and I went to the Montreal Jazz Festival last week. We loved ¹ *it* ____.
Katy and Pat were there, too. We met ² _____ at the B.B. King concert. He is a great guitarist. We're going to see ³ _____ again in New York next month. Do you want to come with ⁴ _____? Do you think Alicia would like to go too? Let's ask ⁵ _____.
I hope we see ⁶ _____ soon.
Best,
Kenny

Vocabulary

7 List adjectives that can go with each noun. Compare answers.

busy	fantastic	long	delicious
small	beautiful	terrible	important
loud	good	big	
exciting	bad	nice	

weather	bad, nice, terrible, good
a person	nice
food	
a day	
music	
a trip	

Recycling Center

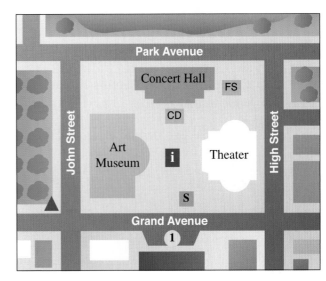

8 Look at this map of a jazz festival site. Write sentences with *on, in front of, between, on the corner of, next to,* or *across from.*

1 Jazz Stage **1**
   The Jazz Stage is on Grand Avenue.

2 Music Store **CD**
   _____

3 Information Center **i**
   _____

4 Food Stand **FS**
   _____

5 Subway Stop **S**
   _____

6 Souvenir Store ▲
   _____

Fun Spot

Use all the letters. Write four celebration words.

a a a a a b d d d d e e g g h i i i i
n n n n o r r r r s t t u v w y y

Example *b i r ...*

104

Keep on talking!

Make a class directory

1 Complete the first section of the address book with your information.

2 Interview two people in your class. Write the information in your book.

> Example A: *What's your name?*
> B: *Danny Chang*
> A: *What's your telephone number?*
> B: *It's…*

3 Share the information with the class. Create a class directory.

Name	
Street Address	
City	
Telephone (home)	
Telephone (work)	
E-mail	
Name	
Street Address	
City	
Telephone (home)	
Telephone (work)	
E-mail	
Name	
Street Address	
City	
Telephone (home)	
Telephone (work)	
E-mail	

Find the conversations

1 Work with a partner. Make two conversations with the sentences below. Then compare answers with another pair. Are they the same?

Here is the beginning of each conversation.

1
A: What time is the movie?
B: *It's at 2:30*.

2
C: Where is the Japanese class?
D: _____

Oh, no, we're late. It's 3 o'clock now.
It's in Room 3.
Yes, you're right. It's 2 o'clock.
But the students are in Room 5.
Look at this schedule. Is this a 3 or a 5?
~~It's at 2:30.~~
No, it isn't. Your watch is wrong.
It's a 5.

2 Cover the conversations and try to remember them. Practice with your partner.

3 Make similar conversations. Use different times, places, and events.

Class	Room	Time
Beginning Japanese	5	5 p.m.
Advanced Spanish	3	7 p.m.

NOW PLAYING
The Message Mystery
2:30   5:00   7:30   10:00

105

Object charts: Student A

(For B's part of this activity, go to page 109.)

1 Work with a partner. **A**, look at the box diagram. Follow these instructions:

    a Write the teacher's name under the newspaper in Box F.
    b Draw a computer on the table in Box C.

2 Work with **B**. Tell **B** about the things in your boxes. Give instructions.

    Example *Write the word* sunglasses *in Box A.*

3 Listen to **B**. Write and draw **B**'s items in your squares. Ask questions if necessary.

    Examples *Can you repeat that? How do you spell…?*

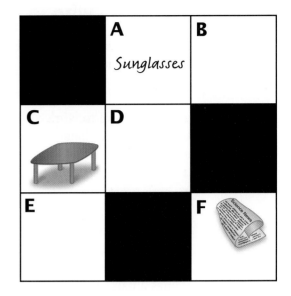

Who's who?

1 Work with a partner. Read the sentences in the box below. Look at the Falon Family Tree. Then fill in the blanks with the missing names.

    Example A: *Hmm. Anna has one granddaughter. I think that her name is Alison.*
                 B: *Yes, that's right. Alison has one brother. His name is…*

Alison is Anna's granddaughter.
Paul has one sister. Her name is Alison.
Ted is Paul's father.
Nancy is Ted's wife.
Joan and Nancy are sisters.
Jack is Conor's son.
Anna is Jack's mother.
Edith is Paul's aunt.
Jack and Edith have one son. His name is Carl.

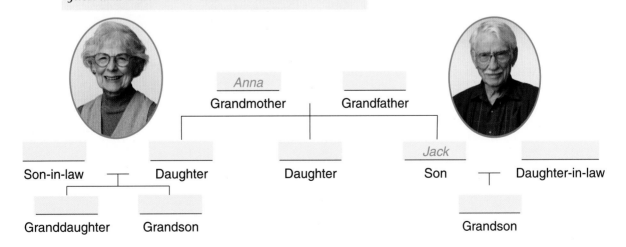

2 Compare your answers with another pair.

6 ▶ Find someone who...

1 Ask other students. Try to find one person for each item. Write the person's name in the space.

Example *Do you wear a suit to work?*

a wears a suit to work   _____
b likes to wear hats   _____
c has a green pen   _____
d wants to buy a computer   _____
e buys a newspaper every day   _____
f reads fashion magazines   _____
g likes black clothes   _____
h likes bright colors for clothes   _____
i has a red or purple shirt   _____
j has a pair of yellow socks   _____
k loves to wear jeans   _____
l likes to shop for clothes   _____

2 Discuss the results with the class.

UNIT

7 ▶ What do you do in the evening?

1 Look at the chart. Which three activities are most popular?

2 Work with a small group. Talk about evening activities. Ask each person for three different activities. Add more activities as necessary. For example, do some people work or study in the evening?

> **Example A:** *Tell me three things you do in the evening.*
> **B:** *Well, I have a class two evenings every week. And then I like to be with my family.*

3 Work with the class. Create a chart for the whole group with statistics about evening activities.

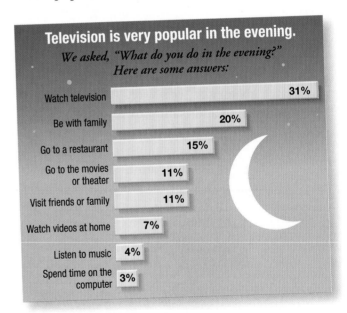

Television is very popular in the evening.

We asked, "What do you do in the evening?" Here are some answers:

Watch television	31%
Be with family	20%
Go to a restaurant	15%
Go to the movies or theater	11%
Visit friends or family	11%
Watch videos at home	7%
Listen to music	4%
Spend time on the computer	3%

UNIT
8 ▶ **The food trip**

Play the game and talk about food.

1 Play in groups. Use one marker for each person and one die.
2 Roll the die and move that number of spaces on the board.
3 When you land on a square with a question or an instruction, answer the question or follow the instruction.
4 If your response is correct, move ahead two spaces. If it is incorrect, move back one. (The group decides if your response is correct or not. If you disagree, ask the teacher.)
5 The person who reaches END first wins the game.

Object charts: Student B

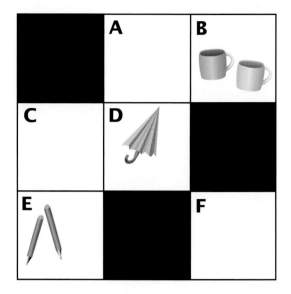

(For A's part of this activity, go to page 106.)

1 Work with a partner. **B**, look at the box diagram. Follow these instructions:

    a Write the word *umbrella* under the umbrella in Box D.

    b Draw a notebook next to the pens in Box E.

2 Work with **A**. Tell **A** about the things in your boxes. Give instructions.

    Example *Draw two coffee mugs in Box B.*

3 Listen to **A**. Write and draw **A**'s items in your squares. Ask questions if necessary.

    Examples *Can you repeat that? How do you spell…?*

Our town: Student A

(For B's part of this activity, go to page 111.)

1 **A**, five places are missing on your map. Ask **B** for the location of these places and write them on your map.

    school   shoe store   bookstore   newsstand   bus stop

    Example A: *Where's the bookstore?*
                    B: *It's on Main Street, next to the bank.*

A

2 Compare maps with your partner. Are the maps the same?

An extreme sport: Student A

(For B's part of this activity, go to page 113.)

1 Read these four sentences from an article about a sporting event called a *triathlon*. Your partner has four sentences from the same article. The sentences are not in logical order.

> The total time for the race is about eight hours for men and nine hours for women.
>
> The race usually starts early, at about 6:30 a.m.
>
> The sports are swimming, cycling, and running.
>
> In race number two, they get on their bikes and ride 112 miles!

2 Work with your partner. Read your sentences. Listen to your partner's sentences. Put the sentences in logical order.

   Here is the first sentence:

   1 *What is a triathlon?* _____   6 _____
   2 _____   7 _____
   3 _____   8 _____
   4 _____   9 _____
   5 _____

What am I doing?

1 Fill in the blanks in the sentence with a) a room in the house and b) an activity. Use the present continuous. Don't show your sentence to other students.

   I'm in the _____, and I'm _____.

   Example   *I'm in the kitchen, and I'm eating pizza.*

2 Work in groups. The other people in your group guess where you are and what you are doing. They can ask only ten *yes / no* questions.

   Example A: *Are you in the living room?*
          B: *No, I'm not.*
          C: *Are you in the kitchen?*
          B: *Yes, I am.*
          D: *Are you cooking?*
          B: *No, I'm not....*

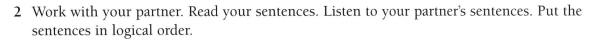

A communication crossword: Student A

(For B's part of this activity, go to page 114.)

1 Work with a partner. **A**, you have the *down* words in this crossword puzzle. Your partner has the *across* words. Help your partner guess the down words. Don't say the words. Give *clues.*

Examples of clues: *Number 4 down is a month. It's before October.* (Answer: SEPTEMBER)

2 Change roles. Listen to your partner's clues for the *across* words. Complete your puzzle.

3 Check your answers with your partner.

Our town: Student B

(For A's part of this activity, go to page 109.)

1 **B**, five places are missing on your map. Ask **A** for the location of these places and put them on your map.

bank   museum   post office   subway stop   café

Example **B**: *Where's the café?*
A: *It's on River Street, next to the grocery store.*

B

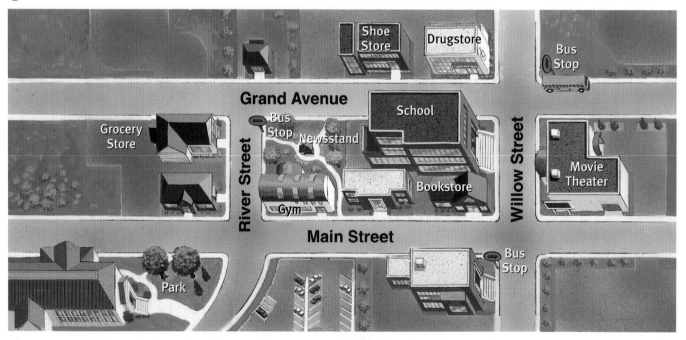

2 Compare maps with your partner. Are the maps the same?

UNIT 13 **Good advice**

Play the game and give good advice.

1 Play in groups. Use one marker for each person and one die.
2 Roll the die and move that number of spaces around the circle.
3 When you land on a square with a problem, make a sentence with *should, shouldn't,* or *don't* and some advice.
4 If your advice is appropriate, move ahead one space. If not, move back two spaces. (The group decides if the advice is appropriate. If you disagree, ask the teacher.)
5 The first person to get to the END square wins the game.

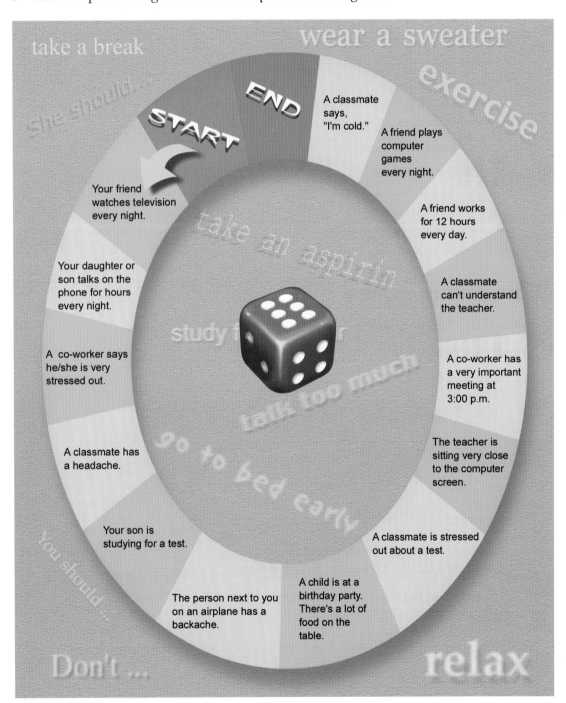

An extreme sport: Student B

(For A's part of this activity, go to page 110.)

1 Read these four sentences from an article about a sporting event called a *triathlon*. Your partner has four sentences from the same article. The sentences are not in logical order.

> In race number three, they run 26.2 miles.
>
> In race number one, the athletes swim 2.4 miles.
>
> In the afternoon after the race, the athletes usually sleep!
>
> A triathlon is a race with three different sports.

2 Work with your partner. Read your sentences. Listen to your partner's sentences. Put the sentences in logical order.

Here is the first sentence:

1 *What is a triathlon?*   6 _____
2 _____   7 _____
3 _____   8 _____
4 _____   9 _____
5 _____

Write your own story

1 Complete this story with your own ideas. Use your imagination.

A Wonderful Vacation.

_____ I went to _____ with
(When?)   (Where?)

_____. We went to _____ and
(Who?)   (Where?)

_____. The weather was _____. We
(Did what?)   (Describe)

met _____. We didn't _____ and I
(Who?)   (What?)

was _____. We came home _____.
(Describe)   (When?)

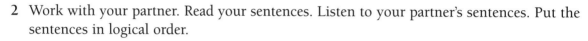

Last year I went to

Example *Last year I went to Paris with my friend Lise. We went to the Louvre and saw…*

2 Practice telling the story to your partner. Add details to make it more interesting.

3 Listen to your partner's story. Use expressions to show your interest.

Examples *Oh, really? Wow! That's interesting!*

4 Work with a new partner. Listen to your partner's story and then tell your story again.

UNIT 12

A communication crossword: Student B

(For A's part of this activity, go to page 111.)

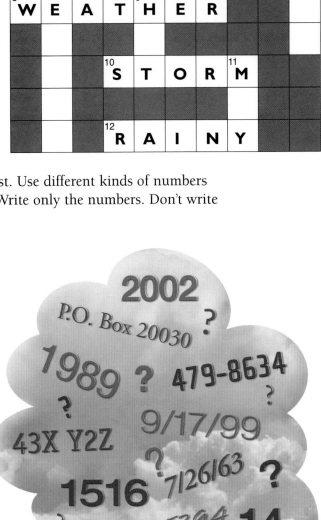

ACROSS →

DOWN ↓

1 Work with a partner. **B**, you have the *across* words in this crossword puzzle. Your partner has the *down* words. Help your partner guess the across words. Don't say the words. Give *clues.*

> Examples of clues: *Number 5 across is a fruit. It is red.*
> (Answer: APPLE)

2 Change roles. Listen to your partner's clues for the *down* words. Complete your puzzle.

3 Check your answers with your partner.

UNIT 15

Numbers in your life

1 Write down five numbers that were important in your life at some time in the past. Use different kinds of numbers (for example, telephone numbers or years). Write only the numbers. Don't write explanations.

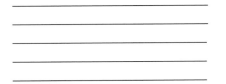

2 Work in small groups. Dictate your number list to the other people in your group.

3 Ask and answer questions about the numbers on your lists.

> Example A: *Why is the number 438-7920 important for you?*
> B: *Well, that was my telephone number in Santiago, Chile.*
> C: *Really! When did you live in Santiago?*
> B: *I lived there in…*

2002
P.O. Box 20030 ?
1989 ? 479-8634
? ?
43X Y2Z 9/17/99
?
1516 7/26/63 ?
? 14
555-681-5394
? ?

Practice your English

1 Work with a partner. Write three ideas for practicing English outside the classroom.

    1 We're going to _____.
    2 _____
    3 _____

2 Compare your ideas with another pair.

3 Make a list with ideas from the whole class. Discuss the ideas. Which are the most practical?

Vocabulary Reference

This section brings together key words and expressions from each unit. Use *Word for Word* to note down other important words that you want to remember.

Countries (*n.*)	Nationalities (*adj.*)	Countries (*n.*)	Nationalities (*adj.*)
Brazil	Brazilian	Kenya	Kenyan
Canada	Canadian	Korea	Korean
China	Chinese	Lebanon	Lebanese
Colombia	Colombian	Mexico	Mexican
Germany	German	Norway	Norwegian
Ireland	Irish	Spain	Spanish
Italy	Italian	the United Kingdom	British
Japan	Japanese	the United States	American

Months (*n.*)
January
February
March
April
May
June
July
August
September
October
November
December

Days (*n.*)
Sunday
Monday
Tuesday
Wednesday
Thursday
Friday
Saturday

Numbers (*n.*)

zero (oh)	twenty-one
one	twenty-two
two	twenty-three
three	twenty-four
four	twenty-five
five	twenty-six
six	twenty-seven
seven	twenty-eight
eight	twenty-nine
nine	thirty
ten	forty
eleven	fifty
twelve	sixty
thirteen	seventy
fourteen	eighty
fifteen	ninety
sixteen	one hundred
seventeen	
eighteen	
nineteen	
twenty	

Ordinal Numbers (*adj.*)
first
second
third
fourth
fifth
sixth
seventh
eighth
ninth
tenth
eleventh
twelfth
thirteenth
fourteenth
fifteenth
sixteenth
seventeenth
eighteenth
nineteenth
twentieth
twenty-first
twenty-second
thirtieth
thirty-first

Unit 1: A world of words

be (*v.*)
boy (*n.*)
camera (*n.*)
common (*adj.*)
country (*n.*)
different (*adj.*)
from (*prep.*)
girl (*n.*)
guitar (*n.*)
he (*pron.*)
I (*pron.*)
introduction (*n.*)
it (*pron.*)
know (*v.*)
man (*n.*)
name (*n.*)
name tag (*n.*)
nationality (*n.*)
obvious (*adj.*)
popular (*adj.*)

she (*pron.*)
they (*pron.*)
tour guide (*n.*)
tourist (*n.*)
we (*pron.*)
woman (*n.*)
world (*n.*)
you (*pron.*)

Expressions
Hello.
Hi.
My name's…
Nice to meet you.
This is…
What's your name?
Where are you from?

Unit 2: Centered on language

address (*n.*)
advanced (*adj.*)
alphabet (*n.*)
apartment (*n.*)
beginning (*adj.*)
book (*n.*)
class (*n.*)
close (*v.*)
computer (*n.*)
conversation (*n.*)
direction (*n.*)
education (*n.*)
e-mail address (*n.*)
form (*n.*)
important (*adj.*)
intermediate (*adj.*)
the Internet (*n.*)
language (*n.*)
language class (*n.*)
last name (*n.*)
level (*n.*)

list (*n.*)
listen (*v.*)
make (*v.*)
movies (*n.*)
not (*adv.*)
notebook (*n.*)
number (*n.*)
open (*v.*)
partner (*n.*)
read (*v.*)
reason (*n.*)
register (*v.*)
room (*n.*)
say (*v.*)
song (*n.*)
spell (*v.*)
student (*n.*)
study (*v.*)
teacher (*n.*)
telephone number (*n.*)
travel (*n.*)

understand (*v.*)
what (*adv.*)
where (*adv.*)
why (*adv.*)
work (*n., v.*)
write (*v.*)

Expressions
Can you repeat
    that?
How do you
    spell…?

117

Unit 3: Take note!

a.m.
at (prep.)
call (v.)
come (v.)
day (n.)
dinner (n.)
door (n.)
face-to-face (adv.)
family (n.)
football (n.)
friend (n.)
go (v.)
grass (n.)
handwritten
   message (n.)
here (adv.)
late (adj.)
lunch (n.)
meeting (n.)
message (n.)

midnight (n.)
noon (n.)
now (adv.)
on (prep.)
p.m.
party (n.)
put (v.)
quiet (adj.)
run (v.)
sign (n.)
sit (v.)
stand (v.)
tennis (n.)
time (n.)
walk (v.)
week (n.)

Expressions
   Excuse me.
   I'm sorry.
   Please
   Thank you
   You're welcome.

Unit 4: Familiar things

address book (n.)
artist (n.)
backpack (n.)
briefcase (n.)
brush (n.)
businessperson (n.)
cat (n.)
chair (n.)
(coffee) mug (n.)
comb (n.)
construction
   worker (n.)
credit card (n.)
desk (n.)
doctor (n.)
envelope (n.)
favorite (adj.)
home (n.)
in (prep.)
job (n.)

keys (n.)
messy (adj.)
neat (adj.)
newspaper (n.)
next to (prep.)
nurse (n.)
object (n.)
on (prep.)
organized (adj.)
pen (n.)
pencil (n.)
picture (n.)
police officer (n.)
stamp (n.)
stethoscope (n.)
sunglasses (n.)
table (n.)
thing (n.)
this / these (dem. adj. /
   pron.)

umbrella (n.)
under (prep.)
useful (adj.)
waiter / waitress (n.)
wallet (n.)
watch (n.)

Unit 5: Family network

aunt (n.)
bicycle (n.)
brother (n.)
brother-in-law (n.)
car (n.)
children (n.)
cousin (n.)
daughter (n.)
do (v.)
dog (n.)
every (adj.)
family reunion (n.)
father (n.)
fun (adj.)
glad (adj.)
grandchildren (n.)
granddaughter (n.)
grandfather (n.)
grandmother (n.)
grandparents (n.)
grandson (n.)

guy (n.)
happy (adj.)
have (v.)
holiday (n.)
house (n.)
husband (n.)
live (v.)
married (adj.)
meet (v.)
month (n.)
mother (n.)
nephew (n.)
nice (adj.)
niece (n.)
often (adv.)
once (n.)
parents (n.)
place (n.)
relationship (n.)
see (v.)
sister (n.)

sister-in-law (n.)
small (adj.)
son (n.)
uncle (n.)
weekend (n.)
wife (n.)

Expressions
Are you from
    around here?
Come on.

Word for Word

Unit 6: Buying power

batteries (n.)
black (adj.)
blue (adj.)
boots (n.)
buy (v.)
cable (n.)
cell phone (n.)
CD (n.)
cent (n.)
clothes (n.)
color (n.)
crowd (n.)
department store (n.)
dollar (n.)
dress (n.)
electrical (adj.)
fitting room (n.)
food (n.)
gray (adj.)
green (adj.)
hat (n.)

help (v.)
home delivery (n.)
item (n.)
jacket (n.)
jeans (n.)
laptop computer (n.)
magazine (n.)
medium (adj.)
need (v.)
online (adv.)
orange (adj.)
order (v., n.)
pants (n.)
printer (n.)
purple (adj.)
red (adj.)
save (v.)
shirt (n.)
shoes (n.)
shop (v.)
shopping (n.)

shopping mall (n.)
shorts (n.)
size (n.)
skirt (n.)
socks (n.)
software (n.)
speak (v.)
store (n.)
suit (n.)
sweater (n.)
that / those (dem.
adj. /
    pron.)
tie (n.)
T-shirt (n.)
wear (v.)
white (adj.)
yellow (adj.)

Expressions
Can I help you?

Can I see…?
Can I take your
    order?
Can I try it on?
How much…?
I'm just looking.
over there

Word for Word

Unit 7: Day in, day out!

about (*prep.*)
actor (*n.*)
architect (*n.*)
article (*n.*)
baby (*n.*)
breakfast (*n.*)
business director (*n.*)
chef (*n.*)
crazy (*adj.*)
daily schedule (*n.*)
deliver (*v.*)
during (*prep.*)
early (*adv.*)
eat (*v.*)
editor (*n.*)
energy (*n.*)
evening (*n.*)
exercise (*n.*)
famous (*adj.*)
finish (*v.*)

from...to (*prep.*)
hospital (*n.*)
hotel (*n.*)
hotel guest (*n.*)
interview (*v.*)
journalist (*n.*)
late (*adv.*)
lunch break (*n.*)
meal time (*n.*)
mile (*n.*)
morning (*n.*)
night (*n.*)
office (*n.*)
package courier (*n.*)
patient (*n.*)
pick up (*v.*)
relax (*v.*)
restaurant (*n.*)
start (*v.*)
tired (*adj.*)

typical (*adj.*)
usually (*adv.*)
when (*adv.*)

Expressions
deliver a baby
deliver a package
get up
go to bed
How interesting.
on call
pick up a package
Really?
That sounds
    interesting.
watch TV
What do you
do?
What time do
    you...?

Unit 8: Essential ingredients

any (*adj.*)
apple (*n.*)
avocado (*n.*)
banana (*n.*)
beans (*n.*)
beef (*n.*)
bread (*n.*)
broccoli (*n.*)
cake (*n.*)
carrot (*n.*)
cheese (*n.*)
chicken (*n.*)
chile pepper (*n.*)
chocolate (*n.*)
cooking (*n.*)
cup (*n.*)
delicious (*adj.*)
dressing (*n.*)
drink (*n., v.*)
fish (*n.*)
flavor (*n.*)

fresh (*adj.*)
fruit (*n.*)
garlic (*n.*)
green pepper (*n.*)
gumbo (*n.*)
hamburger (*n.*)
hot dog (*n.*)
hungry (*adj.*)
influence (*n.*)
ingredient (*n.*)
lemon (*n.*)
lettuce (*n.*)
meat (*n.*)
menu (*n.*)
milk (*n.*)
olive (*n.*)
onion (*n.*)
orange (*n.*)
pie (*n.*)
piece (*n.*)
potato (*n.*)

recipe (*n.*)
rice (*n.*)
roast beef (*n.*)
salad (*n.*)
salad bar (*n.*)
sandwich (*n.*)
sausage (*n.*)
seafood (*n.*)
shopping list (*n.*)
shrimp (*n.*)
soda (*n.*)
some (*adj.*)
soup (*n.*)
spices (*n.*)
spicy (*adj.*)
strawberries (*n.*)
tea (*n.*)
tomato (*n.*)
vegetable (*n.*)
want (*v.*)

Expressions
I'm not hungry.
I'm full.
I'm on a diet.
Would you like...?

Unit 9: In the neighborhood

across (from) (*prep.*)
area (*n.*)
bank (*n.*)
beautiful (*adj.*)
behind (*prep.*)
between (*prep.*)
bookstore (*n.*)
bus stop (*n.*)
café (*n.*)
center (*n.*)
central (*adj.*)
city (*n.*)
community (*n.*)
convention center (*n.*)
difficult (*adj.*)
drugstore (*n.*)
grocery store (*n.*)
harbor (*n.*)
ideal (*adj.*)
in front of (*prep.*)
integrated (*adj.*)

interesting (*adj.*)
like (*v.*)
little (*adj.*)
map (*n.*)
movie theater (*n.*)
museum (*n.*)
near (*prep.*)
neighbor (*n.*)
neighborhood (*n.*)
newsstand (*n.*)
noisy (*adj.*)
on the corner of (*prep.*)
parking lot (*n.*)
post office (*n.*)
quiet (*adj.*)
school (*n.*)
street (*n.*)
suburb (*n.*)
subway stop (*n.*)
theater (*n.*)
think (*v.*)

town (*n.*)
traffic (*n.*)
variety (*n.*)
video store (*n.*)

Unit 10: Fun and games

ability (*n.*)
act (*v.*)
and (*conj.*)
artistic (*adj.*)
athletic (*adj.*)
baseball (*n.*)
basketball (*n.*)
but (*conj.*)
can (*v.*)
computer
  programming (*n.*)
creative (*adj.*)
cook (*v., n.*)
dance (*v.*)
downhill mountain
  biker (*n.*)
draw (*v.*)
drums (*n.*)
far (*adv.*)
fast (*adv.*)
fix (*v.*)

golf (*n.*)
high (*adv.*)
hit (*v.*)
hockey (*n.*)
ice skate (*v.*)
jewelry (*n.*)
jump (*v.*)
kick (*v.*)
lift (*v.*)
mechanical (*adj.*)
motorcycle (*n.*)
or (*conj.*)
paint (*v.*)
photography (*n.*)
piano (*n.*)
play (*v.*)
player (*n.*)
ride (*v.*)
sing (*v.*)
skate (*v.*)
ski (*v.*)

skiing (*n.*)
soccer (*n.*)
speed skater (*n.*)
sport (*n.*)
sprinter (*n.*)
swim (*v.*)
talent (*n.*)
throw (*v.*)
trumpet (*n.*)
volleyball (*n.*)
website design (*n.*)
weightlifter (*n.*)

Expressions
I can teach / show
  you.
I don't know how
  to…
I'll teach / show
  you.
No, thanks.

That'd be great.

Unit 11: Home phone

arrangements (*n.*)
bathroom (*n.*)
bedroom (*n.*)
boyfriend (*n.*)
carry (*v.*)
dining room (*n.*)
drive (*v.*)
furniture (*n.*)
garage (*n.*)
get (*v.*)
invited (*adj.*)
kitchen (*n.*)
living room (*n.*)
move (*v.*)
radio (*n.*)
ring (*v.*)
script (*n.*)
shower (*n.*)
sleep (*v.*)
take (*v.*)

use (*v.*)
work (*v.*)

Expressions
Can I speak to…,
   please?
I'll call back later.
Is…there?
Just a minute.
One moment, please.
take a shower
talk on the phone
This is…
Who's calling, please?

Unit 12: Hot and cold

always (*adv.*)
awful (*adj.*)
beach (*n.*)
cloud (*n.*)
cloudy (*adj.*)
cold (*adj.*)
cool (*adj.*)
definitely (*adv.*)
dust storm (*n.*)
extreme (*adj.*)
fall (*n.*)
fog (*n.*)
foggy (*adj.*)
hardly ever (*adv.*)
horrible (*adj.*)
hot (*adj.*)
long (*adj.*)
lovely (*adj.*)
low (*adj.*)
Mars (*n.*)
mountain (*n.*)

never (*adv.*)
north (*n.*)
often (*adv.*)
possibly (*adv.*)
probably (*adv.*)
rain (*n., v.*)
rainy (*adj.*)
season (*n.*)
small talk (*n.*)
snow (*n., v.*)
snowy (*adj.*)
sometimes (*adv.*)
south (*n.*)
spring (*n.*)
summer (*n.*)
sun (*n.*)
sunny (*adj.*)
temperature (*n.*)
terrible (*adj.*)
vacation (*n.*)
warm (*adj.*)

weather (*n.*)
wind (*n.*)
windy (*adj.*)
winter (*n.*)
wonderful (*adj.*)

Expressions
What a terrible day!
What's the weather
   like?
Lovely day, isn't it?

Unit 13: Take care of yourself

addictive (adj.)
advice (n.)
ailment (n.)
arm (n.)
aspirin (n.)
back (n.)
big (adj.)
body (n.)
careful (adj.)
cold (n.)
comfortable (adj.)
cross (v.)
ear (n.)
eye (n.)
flat (adj.)
floor (n.)
foot / feet (n.)
hand (n.)
head (n.)
headache (n.)
hot liquids (n.)

hurt (v.)
ignore (v.)
kind of (adv.)
knee (n.)
leg (n.)
neck (n.)
not very (adv.)
pretty (adv.)
problem (n.)
really (adv.)
relaxed (adj.)
remedy (n.)
researcher (n.)
screen (n.)
should / shouldn't (v.)
shoulder (n.)
stomachache (n.)
straight (adj.)
stressed out (adj.)
stretch (v.)
support (v.)

tired (adj.)
too (adv.)
try (v.)
turn off (v.)
turn on (v.)
very (adv.)
visual impact (n.)
worried (adj.)

Expressions
go to bed early
I hope you feel
  better.
see a doctor
stay warm
take a break
That's a good
  idea.
What's the
  matter?
Why don't you…?

You're probably right.

Word for Word

Unit 14: It was fantastic!

all (adj.)
answer (n.)
bad (adj.)
boss (n.)
bottle (n.)
busy (adj.)
clean (v.)
closet (n.)
coast (n.)
cruise (n.)
decorate (v.)
distance (n.)
exciting (adj.)
fantastic (adj.)
find (v.)
fisherman (n.)
float (v.)
fun (adj.)
help (v.)
hobby (n.)
last (adj.)

letter (n.)
lucky (adj.)
ocean (n.)
phone book (n.)
postage (n.)
recover (v.)
response (n.)
return (v.)
sea (n.)
sick (adj.)
strange (adj.)
trip (n.)
yesterday (n.)

Expressions
Dear…
Oh really?
Sincerely,…
That's good.
That's too bad.

Word for Word

Unit 15: Extraordinary lives

adventurous (adj.)
be born (v.)
certain (adj.)
charity (n.)
college (n.)
die (v.)
electricity (n.)
fish (v.)
graduate (v.)
hunt (v.)
lodge (n.)
plan (v.)
poor (adj.)
quickly (adv.)
rebuild (v.)
stock market crash (n.)
success (n.)
successful (adj.)
sure (adj.)
teach (v.)

text (n.)
turn out (v.)
university (n.)

Expressions
get a job
get married
have children
I don't know.
I think…
I'm (not) sure…
start school

Unit 16: Let's celebrate!

anniversary (n.)
birthday (n.)
birthday cake (n.)
building (n.)
burn (v.)
card (n.)
celebrate (v.)
celebration (n.)
ceremony (n.)
date (n.)
feast (n.)
festival (n.)
figure (n.)
fire (n.)
future (n.)
get together (v.)
gift certificate (n.)
girlfriend (n.)
graduation (n.)
huge (adj.)
ice sculpture (n.)

music (n.)
next (adj.)
noise (n.)
ordinal numbers (n.)
participate (v.)
picture (n.)
plan (n.)
present (n.)
send (v.)
special (adj.)
surprise (v.)
take part in (v.)
tennis racket (n.)
tomorrow (n.)
wedding (n.)

Expressions
Do you want to…?
give / get presents
have a party
I'd love to.

I'm sorry. I can't.
send a card
Would you like to…?

124

Grammar Reference

This section summarizes the main grammar points presented in this book.

Simple present: *be* — Unit 1

Affirmative

Subject	be		Subject	be	
I	am	a tourist.	We	are	from Italy.
You	are	a student.	You	are	students.
He / She / It	is	from Italy.	They	are	tourists.

Negative

Subject	be + not		Subject	be + not	
I	am not	a student.	We	are not	tourists.
You	are not	a tourist.	You	are not	students.
He / She / It	is not	from Korea.	They	are not	from Italy.

Contractions: *be* (present)

Affirmative

I'm	he's
you're	she's
we're	it's
they're	

Negative

I'm not
he /she isn't *or* he /she's not
it isn't *or* it's not
you aren't *or* you're not
we aren't *or* we're not
they aren't *or* they're not

Simple past: be — Unit 6

Affirmative

Subject	be		Subject	be	
I	was	late.	We	were	happy.
You	were	at work.	You	were	at home.
He / She / It	was	busy.	They	were	famous.

Negative

Subject	be + not		Subject	be + not	
I	was not	late.	We	were not	at home.
You	were not	at home.	You	were not	busy.
He / She / It	was not	happy.	They	were not	late.

Contractions: *be* (past)

Affirmative

There are no contractions for the affirmative forms of *be* in the past.

Negative

I wasn't
he /she / it wasn't
you weren't
we weren't
they weren't

There is / are — Unit 5

Singular		Plural	
There is	a pen on the table.	There are	three pens on the table.
There isn't	a pen on the table.	There aren't	any pens on the table.

Questions		Answers	
Is there	a pen on the table?	Yes, there is.	No, there isn't.
Are there	pens on the table?	Yes, there are.	No, there aren't.

Contractions: *There is* is usually contracted to *There's* in speaking.

Present continuous · Unit 11

Singular			Plural		
Subject	**be**	**Verb + -ing**	**Subject**	**be**	**Verb + -ing**
I	am	working.	We	are	working.
You	are	working.	You	are	working.
He					
She	is	working.	They	are	working.
It					

Negative: *be + not + verb + ing*   He **is not** sleeping. We **are not** eating.

Future: *be going to* · Unit 16

Singular			Plural		
Subject	**be going to**	**Verb**	**Subject**	**be going to**	**Verb**
I	am going to	relax.	We	are going to	relax.
You	are going to	relax.	You	are going to	relax.
He					
She	is going to	relax.	They	are going to	relax.
It					

Negative: *be + not + going to*   **I'm not** going to relax.

Simple present · Unit 5

Singular		Plural	
Subject	**Verb**	**Subject**	**Verb**
I	work.	We	work.
You	work.	You	work.
He			
She	works.	They	work.
It			

Negative: *do / does + not (don't, doesn't) + verb*
He **doesn't work**. We **don't work**.

Simple past · Units 14, 15

Singular		Plural	
Subject	**Verb**	**Subject**	**Verb**
I	worked.	We	worked.
You	worked.	You	worked.
He			
She	worked.	They	worked.
It			

Negative: *did not (didn't) + verb*
They **didn't work** last week.

Use the base form of the verb after the auxiliaries *do*, *does*, and *did*.

Modal auxiliary verbs · Units 10, 13

	Subject	**Modal**	**Verb**	
Ability	Betty	can	ride	a bike.
	Tom	can't	play	golf.
Advice / Suggestions	Athletes	should	drink	a lot of water.
	You	shouldn't	wear	shorts in the winter.

The forms remain the same in all persons: *can / can't / should / shouldn't* + base form of the verb.
The uncontracted form of *can't* is *cannot*. It is used in formal speech and writing.

Questions: *be* (present and past)   Units 2, 4

Wh- *questions*

Question word	Verb	Subject
What	is	your name?
Where	was	his car?

Yes / No *questions*				**Yes / No *answers***		
Verb	**Subject**			**Yes / No**	**Subject**	**Verb**
Are	you	famous?		Yes,	I	am.
Was	the car	red?		No,	it	wasn't.

Questions: Present continuous and *be going to*   Units 1, 16

Wh- *questions*

Question word	be	Subject		
Why	are	you	leaving	early?
When	is	she	going to finish	that book?

Yes / No *questions*				**Yes / No *answers***		
be	**Subject**			**Yes / No**	**Subject**	**Verb**
Is	your brother	sleeping?		No,	he	isn't.
Are	you	going to study?		Yes,	I	am.

Questions: Present, past, *can*, and *should*   Units 2, 5, 7, 10, 13

Wh- *questions*

Question word	Auxiliary	Subject	Verb	
How much	does	it	cost?	
When	did	he	go	home?
Where	can	I	buy	a backpack?
Why	should	we	go	to the doctor?

Yes / No *questions*				**Yes / No *answers***		
Auxiliary	**Subject**	**Verb**		**Yes / No**	**Subject**	**Verb**
Does	she	use	a computer?	Yes,	she	does.
Did	he	lift	weights?	No,	he	didn't.
Can	they	play	tennis?	No,	they	can't.
Should	we	buy	that magazine?	Yes,	you	should.

Note that the basic formula for making questions is the same for all verb tenses.

Countable nouns	Uncountable nouns	Unit 8
How many CDs did you buy last month? I bought **one CD.** Sarah bought **four CDs.**	**How much tea** do you drink? I like **tea** and cookies. My mother drinks **two cups of tea** after dinner.*	

*To "count" an uncountable noun, use an expression of quantity, for example, *two cups of.*

Some	Any	Unit 8
I am going to buy **some** new books today. Rachel ate **some** broccoli for lunch. Did you invite **some** friends over?* Do you want **some** fruit?*	I am **not** going to buy **any** new clothes this week. Michael did**n't** eat **any** lunch yesterday. Do we have **any** tomatoes? Did you get **any** mail today?	

Some is often used in questions for invitations or offers. In other questions use *any.*

Example   *Would you like some coffee? But: Do we have any coffee?*

Pronouns and possessive forms			Units 1, 3, 16
Subject pronouns	*Object pronouns*	*Possessive adjective*	*Possessive 's*
I	me	my	Sally's
you	you	your	John's
he	him	his	
she	her	her	
it	it	its	
we	us	our	
you	you	your	
they	them	their	Sally and John's

To show that a plural noun is possessive, add ' after the final s. *The teachers' books are red.*

Prepositions	Time	Place
		Units 3, 4, 9
across from		✓
at	✓	✓
behind		✓
during	✓	
from...to	✓	✓
in	✓	✓
in front of		✓
near		✓
next to		✓
on	✓	✓

Demonstratives		Unit 6
	As adjectives	*As pronouns*
Near	*This* song is popular.	*This* is a popular song.
	These clothes are old.	*These* are old clothes.
Far	*That* house is large.	*That* is a large house.
	Those buildings are new.	*Those* are new buildings.

Adjectives	Unit 12
He is wearing a *blue* shirt.	His shirt is *blue*.
I have *long* hair.	My hair is *long*.

The adjective can come before the noun it modifies or after *be*.

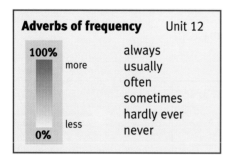

Adverbs of frequency   Unit 12

100% — more — always / usually / often / sometimes / hardly ever — less — 0% never

The position of the adverb of frequency depends on the verb in the sentence.
Be: *She **is always** tired at night.*
Other verbs: *I **always** watch TV at night.*

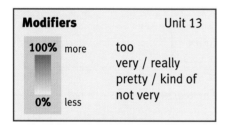

Modifiers   Unit 13

100% more — too / very / really / pretty / kind of / not very — 0% less

Pretty and *kind of* are informal.
The modifier comes before the adjective: *That sandwich is **too** large!*

Irregular Verbs

Base form	Simple past	Base form	Simple past
be	was / were	ride	rode
buy	bought	ring	rang
come	came	run	ran
do	did	say	said
draw	drew	see	saw
drink	drank	sell	sold
drive	drove	send	sent
eat	ate	sing	sang
find	found	sit	sat
get	got	sleep	slept
go	went	stand	stood
have	had	swim	swam
hit	hit	take	took
hurt	hurt	teach	taught
know	knew	think	thought
make	made	throw	threw
meet	met	understand	understood
put	put	wear	wore
read	read	write	wrote

Audioscripts

This section provides audioscripts where a reference and extra support for recorded activities may be helpful.

Unit 1
9a-b

C = Chloe, M1 = Michael #1, M2 = Michael #2

C: Hi, my name's Chloe and this is Michael.
M1: Hi, what's your name?
M2: My name's Michael too.
M1: Well, that's easy! Nice to meet you.
M2: Nice to meet you too.
C: Michael's a really common name, isn't it?
M2: Yes, it is. I think it's common in a lot of different countries. But Chloe isn't really a common name in the United States, is it?
C: No, it isn't. It's an Irish name. So, I think it's common in Ireland.
M2: Hmm, that's interesting.

Unit 2
6

S = Staff, B = Brad

S: OK, Brad, what's your last name?
B: Schultz.
S: How do you spell "Schultz"?
B: S-C-H-U-L-T-Z
S: What's your address?
B: 14 Monroe Street, apartment 4.
S: OK, that's 4 Monroe Street, apartment 14.
B: No, it's 14 Monroe Street, apartment 4.
S: OK. And, what's your phone number?
B: My phone number is 543-2197.
S: And, your e-mail address?
B: Brad123@net.khw
S: Can you repeat that?
B: Brad123@net.khw
S: And, finally, what language class…?
B: Spanish.
S: Beginning…intermediate…advanced?
B: Oh, beginning. I don't know any Spanish.
S: OK, beginning Spanish…

11

Say *student*. / Write *student* in your notebook. / Open your books. / Read the directions. / Listen to the conversation. / Work with a partner. / Close your books.

Unit 3
1b

Sam, the office meeting is at 3 p.m. in conference room A.
Mary, please come to our party. It's on Friday.
Jason, call Ann. Her number is 389-6521.

7a-b

1: Excuse me. What time is it, please?
2: I'm sorry. I don't know.
3: It's 5 o'clock.
1: Thank you.
3: You're welcome.

8b-c

1 Thursday, 10 a.m.
   Hi Matt. It's Alex. Meet me for tennis tomorrow—on Friday—at 4 o'clock as usual. OK? Bye.
2 Thursday, 1:30 p.m.
   Hi Matt. It's Vanessa. Meet me at The Grand Café at 7 o'clock for dinner tonight…. That's 7 o'clock.
3 Thursday, 2:15 p.m.
   Matt, this is Dr. Landau's office. Your appointment is tomorrow…. That's Friday, at 4 o'clock. Goodbye.
4 Thursday, 2:30 p.m.
   Matt, it's Vanessa again. I'm sorry, it isn't The Grand Café for dinner tonight…. It's The Modern Café. Call Jack for the address. His number is 248-9053…. That's 248-9053. Bye.

Unit 4
2a-b

T = Teacher, D = Doctor, C = Construction Worker

T: I'm a teacher, so a lot of these things are useful in my job. A desk and a chair of course...notebooks, pens and pencils—a lot of pens and pencils!—they're useful. A computer is useful for me...and for my students. Yes, all of these things are useful...well, no, not a briefcase...I use a backpack. And my watch is important, too.

D: Let's see.... These aren't the main things for my job. I'm a doctor. But, a desk, chair, and computer are all useful for me. Pens and pencils are useful. Oh yes, and a briefcase is very useful for all my papers.

C: Well, a lot of these things aren't useful...a desk, a chair, a computer. No, they aren't useful for a construction worker like me. Of these things, a pen, pencil, and notebook are useful. Oh, and, a coffee mug. I love coffee!

Unit 5
1c

This is a picture from a party for my parents. They are in the center. Mary is my mother, and Lawrence is my father. This is my sister. Her name is Patti. And this is my brother Calvin. This is Roger. He's my husband. We have two children. Kyra is our daughter, and Danny is our son. Then there's Aunt Loretta. She's my father's sister. Her husband, Uncle Kevin, isn't in the picture. And, finally, this is my sister-in-law Miranda in the corner. She's Calvin's wife.

parents / children / mother / father / son / daughter / sister / brother / aunt / uncle / husband / wife

7a-b

W = Woman, T = Ted

W: So, Ted, are you from around here?

T: No, I'm not. I'm from San Francisco. My parents live there. They're originally from Guangdong Province in China, but they live in San Francisco now.

W: Oh, really. Do you still have family in China?

T: Yes, I do. My mother's parents live in San Francisco. But, my other grandparents—my father's parents—live in China. Some aunts, uncles, and cousins live there too. But I don't know them at all. It's very expensive to travel to China.

W: Yes, I'm sure it is. Do you have brothers or sisters?

T: I have two sisters. I don't have brothers.

W: Do they live in San Francisco?

T: One sister does. Her name's Rita. My other sister, Karen, lives in San Diego.

W: Do you see your family often?

T: Not really. Now that I live in Seattle, I only go to San Francisco about once a month. But, when I'm there, I see my family every day. We have lunch or dinner together. And holidays are important. We always get together on holidays. But, that's enough about me. What about you? Do you have family here?

Unit 6
2a

black / white / green / blue / red / orange / yellow / purple / gray

5a

suit / dress / skirt / shorts / shoes / tie / hat / boots / socks / jeans / jacket / pants / sweater / T-shirt / shirt

12a

W = Woman, P = Mr. Prado

W: OK, Mr. Prado, can I take your order?

P: Yes, item number MB1234, please.

W: OK, that's MB1234, a men's T-shirt.

P: Yes, one of those. Size medium in red, please.

W: OK, one red T-shirt, size medium.

P: Yes.

W: OK, that's $18.95. What's your credit card number?

Unit 7
1a

I get up at 7 a.m.
I start work at 8:30.
I eat lunch at 2:00 p.m.
I finish work at 7:00 or 7:30 p.m.
I have dinner at 9:30 p.m.
I go to bed at 11:30 p.m.

4a-b

K = Kim, D = David

K: What do you do, David?

D: I'm a business director for a hotel company.

K: That sounds interesting. Do you travel a lot?

D: Yes. I visit hotels in different places. Asia, Latin America, and the United States mainly.

K: Hmm. Are hotels different around the world?

D: Well, the big hotels are pretty similar. Nowadays they work hard to satisfy international guests, people from all different countries.

K: Oh? What do you mean?

D: For example, with meal times. People from different countries eat meals at different times. So our hotels take that into consideration.

K: How?

D: We keep the dining room open long hours…all day in fact. Americans usually eat meals early, but Europeans eat meals late.

K: Really?

D: Yes. Often our American guests finish lunch before our European guests even start. Sometimes, the Americans come for dinner and the Europeans aren't even finished with lunch!

K: How interesting. It keeps the cooks busy.

D: Yes, it does.

5a

K = Kim, D = David

K: What do you do, David?

D: I'm a business director for a hotel company.

K: That sounds interesting. Do you travel a lot?

D: What about you Kim? What do you do?

K: I'm a marketing manager.

D: How interesting! Where do you work?

Unit 8

1b

carrots / tomatoes / strawberries / oranges / bread / cheese

1c

The Salad Spot—salads are our specialty!
The salad bar—four kinds of lettuce, broccoli, onions, olives, green peppers, carrots, tomatoes, strawberries, oranges, bread, and cheese
Soup—vegetable soup
Sandwiches—roast beef, chicken
Drinks—coffee, tea, soda

7

K = Kay, A = Alex

K: Alex, this soup is delicious. Is it a new recipe?

A: Yes, it's from this new cookbook I got. Do you really like it?

K: Yes. It has an unusual flavor. Is there a special ingredient?

A: Well, there are two. Can you guess what they are?

K: Hmmm…something a little spicy…spicy hot, that is…. Maybe chile peppers?

A: Yes, that's one ingredient…

K: …but I can't guess the other. What is it?

A: It's cinnamon!

K: Cinnamon? Really? That's unusual.

A: I know, it is. Would you like more?

K: No, thank you. It's very good, but I'm full. I can't eat any more right now.

A: OK, but there's a lot left.

K: Oh, well that's good. We can have some for lunch tomorrow.

8c

1 Would you like a piece of cake?
   No, thanks. I'm on a diet.
2 Would you like a sandwich?
   No, thank you. I'm not hungry.
3 Would you like a cup of coffee?
   Yes, please. Coffee sounds good.
4 Would you like a cup of tea?
   No, thank you. I don't drink tea.

Unit 9

2b

subway stop
bus stop
movie theater
grocery store
bank
drugstore
bookstore
newsstand
post office

7b-c

I live in a really great neighborhood. It has almost everything I need.
There's a bank on the corner of Gold Street and Park Street. There's a nice café called The Star Café next to the bank. I like to go there for a cup of coffee in the morning. Then there's a grocery store next to the café…Devon Market…. There's a parking lot across from the store. And there's a drugstore next to the parking lot. There's also a great little bookstore…Ling's Books…. It's between the drugstore and the post office.
One thing I don't like…there isn't a movie theater…. I wish there was. But…still…I really like this neighborhood.

Unit 10

1b

1 Canada	d ice hockey
2 Germany	f soccer
3 Japan	a baseball
4 Norway	e skiing
5 The Philippines	b basketball
6 Scotland	c golf

The most popular sport in the world is soccer. 20 million people play it in 140 different countries.

8a

D = Diane, T = Tim

D: Do you want to play golf today?

T: Sorry, I don't know how to play golf.

D: That's OK. I'll teach you.

T: Really? That'd be great.

9a-b

D = Dave, M = Melissa

D: Good evening, I'm Dave Malone. Welcome to the game "How much do you know?" It's a game to see how much you really know about a friend or a family member. Tonight we have Melissa and her boyfriend, Louis, on the show. Melissa, you're going to answer questions about Louis. Are you ready?

M: Yes, Dave, I'm ready.

D: Do you think you know Louis well?

M: Yes, I do.

D: OK, first question. Can he cook?

M: That's easy. Yes, he can. He's a really good cook.

D: Correct. OK, next question…. Can he sing?

M: Yes…but not very well.

D: Yes, that's right. That's what Louis says too. OK…next question…. Can he fix your car?

M: No, he can't. He doesn't know anything about cars.

D: Correct. OK, how about sports? Does he like sports?

M: Oh yes, he loves sports.

D: OK, then…. Can he ice skate?

M: Umm…I'm not sure…I don't know. I think he can. He's very athletic. Yes, he can.

D: Are you sure? Is that your answer?

M: Yes, yes it is.

D: Oh no, Melissa. Louis can't ice skate.

M: Oh no…

Unit 11

7a-b

Call 1:

Hello…. Peter? He can't come to the phone right now. He's taking a shower. Can you call back… maybe in about 15 minutes?

Call 2:

Hello…. Oh hi, Linda…. I think Daniela's sleeping right now. She was really tired after work. Can she call you back later?…. OK, what's your number?

Call 3:

Hello…. Yes, Miriam's here. She's watching TV in the living room. Just a minute…

Call 4:

Hello…yes, this is Steve…. Listen, we're eating dinner right now. Can I call you back later… about 8:00? Is that OK?

11b

Call 1

A: Hello.

B: Hi, this is Katrina. Is Ray there?

A: No, he isn't. He's playing golf.

B: OK, I'll call back later.

Call 2

C: Good morning, Block Company.

D: Can I speak to Ms. Galli, please?

C: Who's calling, please?

D: This is Mike Boas.

C: One moment, please.

Unit 12

1a

January / February / March / April / May / June / July / August / September / October / November / December

spring / summer / fall / winter

2a

And now for people traveling in the next few days, here are some January "weather snapshots" so you know what to pack:

Are you going to Stockholm, Sweden? Well, it's typical January weather there…very cold and snowy, so take your winter clothes.

How about Tokyo, Japan? It's cloudy and cool, so take a jacket.

And for those lucky people traveling to Sydney, Australia? It's a perfect January day! Sunny and hot, so pack your bathing suit and plan to go to the beach! That's our travel advisory for today.

6a

1-2 Nice day! Yes, it's beautiful.
3-4 What a terrible day! Yes, it's awful.
5   Lovely day, isn't it? Yes, it is.

Unit 13

2b

H = Host, K = Dr. Kwan

H: Hello, our guest today is Dr. Lia Kwan. Dr. Kwan works with computer-related injuries and problems. Doctor, do you see more computer-related problems these days?

K: Oh definitely, yes. People are doing more and more with computers…and that means more physical problems.

H: So, what can we do?

K: Well, how you sit at the computer is very important.

H: Tell us more.

K: First, have a good chair. It should support your back well.

H: OK, a good chair.

K: Yes. Also, your feet should be flat on the floor when you're sitting. You shouldn't cross your legs.

H: OK. I don't always keep my feet flat on the floor at the computer.

K: I know. It's hard sometimes…. Anyway…you shouldn't sit too close to the screen either. You should sit about an arm's length away.

H: What about the keyboard?

K: The position of arms and hands is also really important. Your arms and hands should be relaxed on the keyboard.

H: That's really helpful. Any other advice?

K: Yes, that's all about sitting. The other thing is about NOT sitting. You shouldn't sit at the computer too long. Make sure you take breaks often and move around too.

Unit 14

4a

A: How was your weekend?
B: It was terrible.
A: Oh really?
B: I was sick all weekend.
A: That's too bad.

C: How was your vacation?
D: It was wonderful.
C: Oh really?
D: Yes, the weather was great and the beaches were beautiful.
C: That's good.

8a

T = Tom, L = Liza

T: Hey, did you ever find out anything about the old letters you found in your apartment?

L: Yes, I did. There's a very old man who lives in the building and I asked him about it.

T: Did he know Clara and Albert?

L: Yes. He said they lived in my apartment for a long time, but they moved about 20 years ago. Unfortunately, he didn't know where they moved.

T: Oh, that's too bad.

L: Yes, but he knew their last name, so I looked in the telephone book. I found someone with the same name and I called.

T: And?

L: I talked to Clara. She was really happy to hear about the letters. She said they were lost when the family moved and she was always sad about that.

T: Hmm.

L: So, I met her last night and returned the letters. We talked for hours and she told me all about the family history.

T: Really?

L: Yes, it was so interesting. Clara was really young, but she and Albert were in love. Then he went to Europe for the war. He wrote letters every week.

T: And then, finally, he came back safely and they were together?

L: Yes…. It's so romantic!

T: Well, it is a nice story.

Unit 15

1b

was born / started school / got a job / got married / had children

2a-b

Justine Kerfoot was born in a suburb of Chicago, Illinois in 1906. Her family had two beautiful houses and a comfortable life in Illinois. Justine planned to stay in Chicago and get a good education. She graduated from college with a degree in zoology, and she planned to go to medical school to become a doctor. Her future seemed very certain. But then the stock market crashed in 1929. The Great Depression came, and suddenly her family didn't have a lot of money. Justine's life changed dramatically. She didn't stay in Chicago and she didn't become a doctor. She didn't live her life as planned.

Unit 16

6a-b

A = Amy, J = Jamie

A: Hi, Jamie. We're talking about what to give Sam for his birthday. Do you have any ideas?

J: Well, I'm not sure. I was thinking about a CD.

A: Not a good idea. Ben's going to give him a CD.

J: OK, well that's out then. Hmm…let's see, what else does he like? Hey, what about something for tennis. He plays a lot of tennis, right?

A: No, not anymore. He stopped because he hurt his arm.

J: Oh…. Well, a book then. A book is always a good present.

A: He doesn't like reading very much.

J: Wow, he's difficult to buy a present for, isn't he?

A: Yes, he is.

J: Well, what are you going to get him, Amy?

A: I don't know. I'm trying to think of something too.

J: Hey, I have an idea. What about a gift certificate? Then he can buy whatever he wants.

A: That is a good idea…. But, wait a minute. I still don't have anything to give him.

J: Don't worry…. It can be from both of us.

A: OK. Great!

Text Acknowledgments

The publishers are grateful to the individuals and institutions named below for permission to include their materials in this book.

p. 6: Names based on statistical information 1995–1999.

p. 57: Vermillion used by permission of Nate Bowman. New Urbanism Principles used by permission of Andres Duany of Duany Plater-Zyberk.

p. 59: "#1 Sport Worldwide." Factmonster.com. ©2000 Learning Network. http://www.factmonster.com/ipka/A0769918.html (October 19, 2001).

p. 76: Lyric of "Blue Skies" by Irving Berlin.
Copyright ©1926, 1927 by Irving Berlin
Copyright Renewed International Copyright Secured
All Rights Reserved Reprinted by Permission

p. 89: "Winds and tides toss up retiree's messages on distant shores" by Bill Murphy. *Sandia Lab News,* June 4, 1999.

p. 93: Justine Kerfoot and Gunflint Lodge used by permission of Jennifer Walsh of Gunflint Lodge.

p. 102: "Celebrate Our Love"
Music & lyrics by Eelke Kalberg ("Kalmani") and Sebastiaan Molijn ("Pronti")
©2000 by Kalberg Publishing and Molijn Publishing

OXFORD
UNIVERSITY PRESS

198 Madison Avenue
New York, NY 10016 USA

Great Clarendon Street
Oxford OX2 6DP England

Oxford   New York
Auckland Bangkok Buenos Aires Cape Town Chennai
Dar es Salaam Delhi Hong Kong Istanbul Karachi Kolkata
Kuala Lumpur Madrid Melbourne Mexico City Mumbai Nairobi
São Paulo Shanghai Taipei Tokyo Toronto

OXFORD is a trademark of Oxford University Press.

ISBN 0-19-463667-X

Copyright © 2003 Oxford University Press

Library of Congress Cataloging-in-Publication Data

Naber, Therese.
  English knowhow. Student book opener / Therese Naber, Angela Blackwell ; with
Michelle Johnstone.
    p. cm.
  ISBN 0-19-453667-X (pbk.)
  1. English language—Textbooks for foreign speakers. I. Title: English knowhow student
book opener. II. Title: Student book opener. III. Blackwell, Angela Glover. IV. Johnstone,
Michelle. V. Title.
PE1128.N24 2003
428.2'4—dc21

                     2003042021

Editor: Margaret Brooks
Associate Editor: Carol Balistreri
Assistant Editor: Alexis Vega-Singer
Design Project Manager: Maria Epes
Series and Cover Designer: Claudia Carlson
Designers: Claudia Carlson, Lyndall Culbertson
Art Editor: Jodi Waxman
Production Manager: Shanta Persaud
Production Coordinator: Eve Wong

Printing (last digit): 10 9 8 7 6 5 4 3 2 1

Printed in Hong Kong.

Acknowledgments

Cover photographs: Eyewire (library); Larry Lawfer/Index Stock (woman on phone);
PictureArts Corporation (trophy); VCG-Taxi/Getty Images (straphanger)

Illustrations: Silke Bachmann/Illustration Web p. 56 (maps); Nick Backes/American Artists
Rep. Inc. pp. 35 (advertisement), 38 (advertisement), 51 (check-in), 52 (gift shop), 59
(athletes), 67 (women), 79 (interview), 86 (couple/thought bubble), 115 (magazines,
computer screen, man, note, video store); Barbara Bastian pp. 13 (invitation, message,
memo), 25 (schedule), 28 (family reunions), 49 (U.S. food), 58 (advertisement), 62
(instructor profile), 71 (seasons), 79 (Do/Don't), 91 (background, stock market crash), 93
(a true pioneer), 100 (invitations), 103 (Montreal, FAQs); Keith Batchellor pp. 2
(businesspeople, tour, picnic), 16 (people), 48 (women), 63 (people), 73 (joggers, rainy
day, businesspeople), 81 (people), 86 (two couples); Kenneth Batelman pp. 34 (cables), 53
(map key), 57 (maps, New Urbanism), 59 (quiz), 60 (amazing athletes), 72 (map), 84
(advice columns), 98 (interviews), 104 (map); Annie Bissett pp. 16 (agenda, messages), 38
(order forms), 51 (form), 52 (form), 64 (questionnaire, forms), 105 (address book, times),
107 (bar graph), 114 (numbers); John Clarke pp. 4 (ailments/remedies), 80 (ailments/
remedies); Lyndall Culbertson p. 7 (brochure, background), 14 (signs), 15 (chart), 17 (notes), 35
(ad layout), 38 (ad layout), 55 (boxes), 71 (TV set), 76 (song), 77 (postcard), 81 (mind
maps), 89 (message in a bottle), 90 (note), 100 (chart, invitations), 102 (song), 106 & 109
(box with illustrations), 111 & 114 (crossword puzzle); Jim DeLapine pp. 15 (clocks), 23
(briefcases), 27 (notebook), 39 (everyday activities), 66 (answering machine and message),
106 (family tree); Bill Dodge p. 23 (cat); Chuck Gillies pp. 3 (people), 22 (people), 34
(shopping scenes), 46 (salad bar), 87 (woman), 88 (women); John Gurney/Bernstein &
Andriulli Inc. pp. 24 (desks), 26 (objects), 70 (clapperboard); Robert Hynes pp. 14 (bike
riding, library), 25 (tour guide), 77 (women), 91 (life events), 107 (people), 110 (people);
Daniel Kirk/Bernstein & Andriulli Inc. pp. 19 (objects), 23 (backpacks, table, chair), 33
(colors, cell phones), 99 (objects); Uldis Klavins pp. 109 & 111 (map); Karen Minot pp. 9
(registration forms), 18 (e-mails), 19 (chart), 37 (article), 48 (notepage), 55 (postcard), 66
(e-mail), 76 (notepad), 82 (computers), 87 (letter), 88 (notepad); Roger Motzkus pp. 9
(people), 10 (people), 30 (people), 36 (people), 55 (people, map), 68 (people), 85 (people
talking), 94 (people); Eric Mueller pp. 31 (objects), 70 (objects); Ortelius Design Inc. pp. 31 (map), 49
(map), 58 (map); Rob Schuster pp. 6 (names, chart), 10 (class lists), 18 (notepad), 42
(everyday living), 50 (chart), 65 (floor plan), 74 (Mars), 96 (profile), 104 (notes); Michael
Stepanek p. 61 (athletes); Don Stewart pp. 64 (game show), 83 (men); Studio Liddell/
American Artists Rep. Inc. pp. 45 (menu), 47 (pantry), 108 & 112 (game, dice); William
Waitzman pp. 11 (students), 13 (people), 20 (man), 37 (people), 56 (people), 66 (Jim)

Commissioned photographs: Arnold Katz Photography pp. 17 (man, woman), 21 (duffle
bag), 45 (salad bar), 47 (supermarket), 48 (spices); Lyndall Culbertson/Oxford University
Press pp. 7 (header, keypad), 13 (door sign, crosswalk signal, header), 71 (header); Mary
Martin p. 42 (Kathryn Flory); Kathryn L. O'Dell/Oxford University Press p. 62 (Richie
Travers); Jodi Waxman/Oxford University Press p. 58 (street)

The publishers would like to thank the following for their permission to reproduce photographs:
Agpix p. 101 (Vasant Panchami); Ping Amranand/SuperStock p. 1 (Hong Kong);
Awestruck/Agpix p. 113 (cycling); Linda Holt Ayriss/Getty Images p. 45 (potatoes); David
Ball/Index Stock p. 90 (Crete); Miwako Ball/International Stock p. 45 (carrots); Scott T.
Baxter/PhotoDisc p. 97 (anniversary); John Bechtold Studio/International Stock p. 76
(man); Walter Bibikow/Index Stock p. 71 (Japan); Christopher Bissell/Taxi p. 33
(shopping); Mark Bolster/ International Stock p. 7 (man); Werner Bokelberg/Getty Images
p. 42 (journalist); Brian Bowman p. 57 (Vermillion: house, street, building); Keith
Brofsky/PhotoDisc p. 85 (woman at work); Thomas Brummett/PhotoDisc p. 97 (header);
David Buffington/PhotoDisc p. 79 (header); C Squared Studios/PhotoDisc p. 49 (soup);
Peter Cade/Getty Images p. 102 (couple on beach); Scott Campbell/International Stock
p. 19 (doctor/nurse); Color Day Production/Getty Images p. 33 (CDs); Comstock p. 71
(spring); Corbis p. 1 (newsstand); James Davis/ International Stock pp. 6 (family), 19
(businessperson); Donna Day/PhotoDisc p. 99 (people); Maria De Kord/International Stock
p. 24 (businessperson); Tony Demin/International Stock p. 85 (rafting); Stephen Derr/Getty
Images p. 33 (books); Prisma Dia/Index Stock p. 32 (family/snow); Digital Vision/Getty
Images p. 50 (food); Jeffrey Dunn/Index Stock p. 24 (woman); Kenneth Ehlers/
International Stock p. 71 (winter, Sweden); ElektrVision AG/Index Stock pp. 85 (header),
91 (header); Eyewire p. 53 (header); Eyewire Collection/Getty Images p. 60 (mountain
biker); Eyewire Collection/PhotoDisc p. 45 (oranges); Gala/SuperStock p. 1 (Paris);
Glasheen Graphics/Index Stock p. 54 (town); Tom and Michele Grimm/International Stock
p. 41 (outside hotel); Charles Gupton Photography/Corbis p. 33 (computer); Tim
Heneghan /Index Stock p. 90 (Alaska); David Hiller/PhotoDisc p. 19 (police officer); Holly
Hitzmen/Index Stock p. 49 (gumbo); Walter Hodges/Corbis p. 24 (student); Marty Honig/
PhotoDisc p. 45 (strawberries); Mitch Hrdlicka/PhotoDisc p. 45 (rice); Image100/Royalty-
Free/Corbis Stock Market pp. 31 (couple), 33 (clothes); ImageState pp. 71 (fall), 84
(woman); Index Stock pp. 25 (Hollywood), 48 (chiles, seafood), 60 (weightlifter);
International Stock p. 28 (family on right); International Stock Photo. Ltd./International
Stock p. 45 (cheese); Shawn Johnston/Fair Street New Media p. 53 (street); Shizuo
Kambayashi (AP staff)/Associated Press p. 101 (Sapporo Yuki Matsuri); Michael Keller/
Index Stock p. 65 (French woman); Richard Kolker/Taxi p. 13 (header); Dennis Lane/
Index Stock p. 75 (park); Peter Langone Inc./International Stock p. 19 (waiter); John
Lawrence/International Stock p. 39 (Madrid); David Lees/FPG p. 85 (party); Ryan McVay/
Getty Images p. 21 (keyring); Ryan McVay/PhotoDisc p. 5 (two adults), 39 (airport,
header); Steve Mason/PhotoDisc p. 5 (four adults); Masterfile p. 77 (Chicago); Rob
Melnychuk/PhotoDisc p. 19 (construction worker); Randy Montoya/Sandia Lab News p. 89
(Harold Myers); Martine Mouchy/Getty Images p. 44 (morning); Stephen B. Myers/
International Stock p. 45 (tomatoes); Nasa.com p. 74 (Mars, dust clouds); Mark
Newman/International Stock p. 71 (Australia); O'Brien/International Stock p. 12 (marquee);
Orion/International Stock p. 71 (summer); Scott Payne/FoodPix p. 41 (inside hotel); Kevin
Peterson/PhotoDisc p. 106 (woman); PhotoDisc pp. 1 (header), 17 (couple), 27 (header),
33 (food), 45 (header), 59 (header), 60 (sprinter), 65 (header), 98 (man), 106 (man);
Phyllis Picardi/International Stock p. 65 (Asian woman); Joe Polillio/Getty Images p. 29
(man); Peter Poulides/Getty Images p. 42 (courier); Patrick Ramsey/International Stock
p. 65 (man); Reuters NewMedia Inc./Corbis Stock Market p. 110 (swimming); Don
Romero Photography/International Stock p. 97 (graduation); Frank Siteman/Index Stock
p. 75 (reading); Ariel Skelley/Corbis p. 27 (family); Don Smetzer/Stone p. 32
(family/cards); Joseph Sohm/ChromoSohm Inc./Corbis p. 12 (airport); Phillip Spears/Getty
Images p. 65 (header); Bill Stanton/International Stock p. 39 (New York); Stockbyte p. 21
(umbrella); Johnny Stockshooter/International Stock p. 54 (city); Superstock p. 28
(families on left and in middle); Svoboda Stock/International Stock pp. 45 (lemons,
bananas, bread), 49 (salad); Table Mesa Productions/David L./Index Stock p. 75 (biking);
Jay Thomas/International Stock p. 19 (teacher); Mike Timo/Getty Images p. 44 (night);
Don Tremain/PhotoDisc p. 97 (wedding); Rudi Von Briel/Index Stock p. 98 (woman); Karl
Weatherly/PhotoDisc p. 60 (speed skaters); Ken Weingart/International Stock p. 69 (cello);
Charles Westerman/International Stock p. 43 (chef); Larry Williams/ Corbis Stock Market
p. 82 (man); Russell Willison/International Stock p. 69 (couple on couch); Mr. John T.
Wong/Index Stock p. 103 (musician); webshots p. 78 (Chicago); Yellow Dog Productions/
Getty Images p. 97 (birthday)

Special thanks to: Cathy Dodge p. 42 (journalist); Kathryn Flory p. 42 (doctor); City Cafe
Coffee Bar p. 45 (salad bar); Gristede's #99 NYC p. 47 (supermarket); Richard Hussan p.
62 ("can do" man); Peter Cockroft p. 71 (weatherman); the Tourist Office of Spain in New
York p. 101 (Las Fallas); the Kerfoot family pp. 91 (Justine Kerfoot, Gunflint Lodge), 93
(dogsled, canoeing, fishing)

*The authors and publishers extend thanks to the following English Language Teaching
professionals and institutions for their invaluable support and feedback during the development
of this series:* Gill Adams (Brazil); Virgílio Almeida and staff (Brazil); Barbara Bangle
(Mexico); Vera Berk (Brazil); James Boyd (Japan); Bonnie Brown de Masis (Costa Rica);
Janaína Cardoso and staff (Brazil); Hector Castillo (Mexico); Dr. Robin Chapman (Japan);
Ana Isabel Delgado (Brazil); Nora Díaz (Mexico); Maria da Graça Duarte and staff (Brazil);
Stephen Edmunds (Mexico); Israel Escalante (Mexico); Raquel Farias and staff (Brazil);
Verónica Galván (Mexico); Saul Santos García (Mexico); Carmen Gehrke and staff (Brazil);
Arlete Würschig Gonçalves and staff (Brazil); Kimberley Humphries (Mexico); Michelle
Johnstone (Canada); Jean-Pierre Louvrier (Brazil); Shan-jen Amy Lu (Taiwan); Mary Meyer
(Paraguay); Dulce Montes de Oca (Mexico); Harold Murillo (Colombia); Connie Reyes
(Mexico); Carmen Oliveira and staff (Brazil); Thelma Félix Oliveira (Brazil); Eliane Cunha
Peixoto and staff (Brazil); Verónica Olguín (Mexico); Claudia Otake (Mexico); Nicola
Sarjeant (Korea); Débora Schisler and staff (Brazil); Lilian Munhoz Soares and staff (Brazil);
Sharon Springer (Costa Rica); Silvia Thalacker and staff (Brazil); Kris Vicca (Taiwan);
Daniel Zarate (Mexico).
Centro Cultural Brasil-Estados Unidos, Santos; Centro de Línguas Estrangeiras Mackenzie,
São Paulo; ENEP Acatlán, Edo. de México; English Forever, Salvador; Escola Técnica
Estadual Fernando Prestes, Sorocaba; GreenSystem, Belo Horizonte; Instituto Cultural
Brasil Norte-Americano, Porto Alegre; MAI, Belo Horizonte; Plus!, Brasília; Quatrum, Porto
Alegre; SENAC Rio; Seven, São Paulo; Talkative, São Paulo; Universidad Autónoma de
México; Universidad Autónoma del Estado de México; Universidade Católica de Brasília;
Universidad La Salle, León, Guanajuato; Universidad Latino Americano, Mexico City;
Universidad Nacional Autónoma de México